D0983048

A History of
Christian Spirituality

A
HISTORY OF
CHRISTIAN
SPIRITUALITY

An Analytical Introduction

Urban T. Holmes, III

The Seabury Press · New York

For Jane

1980
The Seabury Press
815 Second Avenue · New York, N.Y. 10017

Library of Congress Cataloging in Publication Data
Holmes, Urban Tigner, 1930–
A history of Christian spirituality.

Bibliography: p.
Includes index.
1. Spiritual life—History of doctrines.
I. Title.
BV4490.H63   248   80-12870
ISBN 0-8164-0141-1

Contents

Introduction 1

Prayer as a Human Act 1

A Phenomenology of Prayer 3

A Psychology of Prayer 5

An Anthropology of Prayer 7

A Sociology of Prayer 8

The Identification of
Images 11

Issues in Spiritual Reading 12

I. The Early Church 14

Jewish Antecedents 14

  Philo 16

New Testament 17

  John the Baptist 17

  Jesus 17

  Kierkegaard 17

  Paul 18

The Apostolic Fathers 20

  Barnabas 21

  Shepherd of Hermas 21

  Tatian 21

  Ignatius of Antioch 22

  Irenaeus 22

Alexandrian School 23

  Clement of Alexandria 25

  Origen 26

Monasticism 29

  Evagrius Ponticus 30

  Plato 30

  Climacus 30

The Cappadocians 31

  Gregory of Nyssa 31

Monasticism Again 35

  Macarius 35

  Evagrius Ponticus 36

  Climacus 37

  Isaac of Nineveh 38

Dionysius the
Pseudo-Areopagite 39

Reaction to Mysticism 40

  John Chrysostom 41

  Synesius of Cyrene 41

The Ancient West   42

   Ambrose   43

   Augustine   43

   Cassian   45

  ◦ Benedict of Nursia   46

II. The Middle Ages (500–1000)   48

Heroic Age (500–1000)   48

   Gregory the Great   48

   Isidore   49

   Bede the Venerable   49

   Maximus the Confessor   49

   Rabanus Maurus   51

   Chrodegang of Metz   52

   John Scotus or Erigena   52

The High Middle Ages (1000–1300)   54

   Carthusians (Brune)   54

   Guigo II   54

   John of Fecamp   54

   Anselm   55

   Citeaux   55

   Bernard of Clairvaux   55

   William of St. Thierry   57

   Aelred of Rievaulx   59

The Schoolmen   60

   Hugh of St. Victor   61

   Richard of St. Victor   62

Popular Piety   64

The Friars   65

   Francis of Assisi   65

   Bonaventure   66

   Raymond Lull   67

   Dominic   68

   Thomas Aquinas   68

The Late Middle Ages (1300–1500)   70

The Rhineland Mystics   70

   Beguines   71

   Beatrice of Nazareth   71

   Hadiwijch of Antwerp   71

   Meister Eckhart   72

   John Tauler   72

   Henry Suso   75

   John Ruysbroeck   75

   The Cloud of Unknowing   76

The English Mystics   77

   Richard Rolle   77

  ◦ *The Cloud of Unknowing*   79

  ◦ Julian of Norwich   80

   Walter Hilton   81

   Margery Kempe   82

The Fifteenth-Century Demise   83

   Pietism   83

   Gerard Groote   84

   Thomas à Kempis   85

   John Gerson   86

   Catherine of Genoa   87

III. Byzantine Spirituality   89

Sinaitic Monasticism   90

Studite Monasticism   90

   Simeon the New Theologian   90

   Gregory Palamas   91

IV. The Modern Period   93

The Spanish School   93

  Ignatius Loyola   93

  Teresa of Avila   93

  John of the Cross   93

  Garcia Ximenes
  de Cisneros   93

The Italian School   103

  Luis de Molina   104

  Jerome Savonarola   104

  Cajetan   104

  Robert Bellarmine   104

  Lawrence Scupoli   104

The French School   105

  Francis de Sales   105

  Jeanne de Chantal   106

  Clare   106

  Miguel de Molinos   107

  Francis Fenelon   107

  Cardinal Richelieu   108

  Pierre de Berulle   108

  Philip Neri   108

  Cornelius Jansen   108

  Jean-Jacques Olier   108

  John Eudes   109

  Blaise Pascal   110

The English School   112

  Dom Augustine Baker   112

  Richard Hooker   112

  Mainstream
  Anglicanism   113

  John Donne   114

  Lancelot Andrewes   116

  Jeremy Taylor   117

  George Herbert   118

  Nicholas Ferrar   121

  William Law   122

Classical Protestantism   124

  Martin Luther   125

  John Calvin   127

  Jacob Boehme   128

  Francis Rous   130

  Thomas Goodwin   131

  Richard Baxter   131

  John Bunyan   132

Radical Protestantism   134

  Thomas Münzer   134

  George Fox   135

Pietism   136

  Phillipp Jakob Spener   136

  Johann Arndt   136

  August Hermann
  Francke   138

  Jonathan Edwards   138

  George Whitefield   139

  John Woolman   139

  Ludwig Graf
  von Zinzendorf   140

  John Wesley   140

Sparks Among the
Stubble   143

  Albrech Ritschl   143

  Gerhard Tersteegen   143

  William Wilberforce   144

  John Keble   144

  Edward Pusey   144

John Henry Newman   144

Jean-Baptiste
Marie Vianney   144

Therese of Lisieux   144

Gerard Manley
Hopkins   145

Friederich von Hügel   145

Nicodemus of
the Holy Mountain   146

Theophan the Recluse   147

Evelyn Underhill   148

The Contemporary Scene   150

Simone Weil   151

Dag Hammerskjöld   152

Thomas Merton   153

Martin Luther King   155

Conclusion   157

Index of Names   162

Foreword

This book is the result of finding nothing to recommend to my students as an introduction to the wide variety and great richness of the Christian spiritual experience. There is never time in class to do anything but mention a few highlights, and the texts available are either too detailed, too unbalanced, or both. So I have tried my hand at a relatively new venture for me.

In developing the manuscript I am deeply indebted to Harry Pritchett, who taught spiritual theology with me at the School of Theology for four years, and to Sr. Rachel Hosmer, OSH, who read and criticized the manuscript. John Westerhoff also urged me to complete the task of writing. I appreciate Bob Gilday's interest in this work and his encouragement of its revision.

Perhaps my greatest debt, however, is to my students, both undergraduate and graduate. I must also mention with heartfelt thanks those in my graduate seminar on mystical theology who listened, responded, and did a significant portion of the research. They were Steve Harris, Wendy Williams, Don Lavallee, Murillo Bonaby, Hunter Horgan, Bill Buice, Jim Horton, Bob Jewett, Kerry Robb, Mark Engle, and Lew Heigham. If some of you recognize the name of their parish priest in this number, it is no coincidence. These are my students in the Doctor of Ministry program.

Thanks are also in order to Mary Lynn Floore who typed and pieced together the final manuscript.

Urban T. Holmes
Feast of Thomas à Kempis, 1979

Introduction

Prayer As a Human Act

Human beings are spiritual creatures. The word "spirit" comes from a word meaning "breath." The presence of life, and therefore God, has been associated with breath through much of humanity's evolution of consciousness. After all, when we die the breath goes out of us. We exhale, never to inhale again. God, as the life-giving presence, lives in us—or so humankind has thought. So, to say that human beings are spiritual creatures is to suggest that they are capable of possessing the presence of the life-giving God. As one ancient proverb puts it, "To breathe is to pray."

But to be spiritual means more than to be capable of receiving God into our lives. It means that we are called to know God. One way of describing the act of knowing is to say that to be human is to be a *hearer* of the Word of God. Be careful how we think of the "Word of God." Here it means no more than God's self-disclosure. God communicates himself to us and we can receive that communication. *How* we receive that communication is another question. The fourth evangelist tells us that Jesus said, "The wind blows where it wills, and you hear the sound of it, but you do not know whence it comes or whither it goes; so it is with everyone born of the Spirit" (Jn. 3:8). John of the Cross, in

1

the sixteenth century, comments on this by saying that the Word of God is the effect upon the soul.

The effect is, of course, our growth into a closer relationship with God through the power of the Spirit, God inviting us into the whole life. We are "unfinished" humans until we consent to that power of the Spirit and are drawn into a wholeness of being. But we must be careful before we judge too quickly what it is like to be drawn or solicited into fulfillment by God. Christian spiritual masters through the centuries have had different ways of describing that process.

All the spiritual masters say that it involves a relationship between God and humanity that we call prayer. For us, to pray is to intend to hear God and to respond to God. God is absolutely present to *all* people. Prayer does not "make" him present. Prayer is not a work. It begins with our consent to enter into a relationship to which God invites everyone. Prayer is a consent that is grounded in the expectation that God speaks to us and we can hear. This expectation is what is meant by faith.

But humankind is not only spiritual. It is historical. This means more than that we have a past of which we are aware, or even that thinking about the past gives us a sense of the future. To be historical means that by virtue of our reflection on the past we are aware that as humans we live within a flow of time in a finite world in which the one constant is change. Humanity always hears the Word of God within humanity's historical context. God *in himself* is infinite and ineffable. But we only know God as he is to us, who are historical creatures.

This explains why we can believe that the ruthless God of Joshua has some relation with the loving God of Jesus. It is not that God changes. It is our way of understanding God as he is to us that changes. To understand humanity as historical is, therefore, helpful; but it explains why Christian spiritual masters can talk of the spiritual in such different ways. But it also makes the problem of language vital.

Humanity is its language. Language is the means by which we

make sense of our experience and remember it. We speak of God, and in so doing identify, clarify, and share the experience of God. But language is historical. There is always a longing in persons of deep prayer to get behind the finite forms of language to the infinite God, who is ineffable—i.e., he cannot be described by language. This tension exists in any experience of prayer. The mystics will say to us that they cannot describe what they have experienced. Yet they try, and it is never enough.

We are asking the question in this book: *How has Christian humanity throughout its history understood what it is to seek God and to know him?* In asking, we know that this is the only way to get an overview, and yet we are aware that it is the penultimate question. We can never know so as to put in words what it is to see God face to face.

But there is value in the answer we can give to the question. The answer should (1) broaden the limitations of our own horizons; (2) free us to seek a pattern of discipline in the spiritual life that is most suitable to our own life-style; (3) enable us to help others without demanding that they be like us; (4) enlighten and inspire us by the examples of those who have practiced the presence of God in heroic ways—by the "hero" is meant that person who in word and action illumines our consciousness, makes us more aware of who we are in the world and before God; and (5) enhance our skills that we might become competent spiritual guides or companions to others. In other words, the purpose of an historical analysis in spiritual theology is to provide the data for an interpretation of the tradition of Christian spirituality not for its own sake alone, but to enable today's Christian to illumine his or her contemporary meaning of the experience of God in a manner that is meaningful and true.

A Phenomenology of Prayer

It is very important to have a way of describing what patterns of Christian spirituality "look like." When it is possible to develop such a description we discover that there are many options to the shape and flow of our relationship with God and we can identify our own place within the much wider Christian tradition. To this end a phenomenology of prayer is helpful.

Two scales will be applied to the material of Christian spirituality. The horizontal scale is the apophatic/kataphatic scale. Briefly, this raises the question of the degree to which the ascetical method advocates an emptying (apophatic) technique of meditation or an imaginal (kataphatic) technique of meditation.

The vertical scale is the speculative/affective scale. Briefly, this raises the question of whether the spiritual method emphasizes the illumination of the mind (speculative) or the heart or emotions (affective).

By the use of these two scales it is possible to make comparisons between spiritual masters of the church and to define spiritual practice and its immediate objectives with some clarity—the assumption being that in all methods the ultimate goal is union with God. We can speak of options without being judgmental.

We can also use this phenomenology of prayer on the apophatic/kataphatic and speculative/affective scales to distinguish certain dangers of exaggeration. On the accompanying figure, not

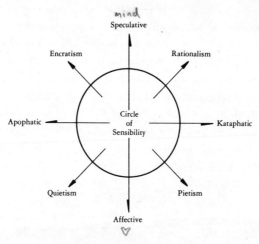

A Phenomenology of Prayer

only have the two scales been defined but a *circle of sensibility* has been identified. Most forms of Christian spirituality will emphasize one of the four possibilities within these scales: apophatic/speculative, speculative/kataphatic, kataphatic/affective, or affective/apophatic. A sensitive spirituality will, however, maintain a certain tension with those other dimensions that are not emphasized as a corrective to an exaggerated form of prayer. "Sensibility" defines for us that sensitivity to the ambiguity of styles of prayer and the possibilities for a creative dialogue within the person and within the community as it seeks to understand the experience of God and its meaning for our world. Without that tension we fall into excesses, which are defined here as encratism, rationalism, pietism, and quietism. From time to time in this survey we will call attention to a risk within certain spiritual masters.

A Psychology of Prayer

The theory of bimodal consciousness is a helpful heuristic model to understand what happens within the human mind in authentic prayer. Bimodal consciousness is the theory that there are two discrete yet interrelated ways in which people make sense of their experience. This is described in some detail in *The Priest in Community* by Urban T. Holmes (Seabury, 1978), pages 9–34; or in *Symposium on Consciousness,* Robert E. Ornstein, ed. (Penguin Books, 1977), pages 26–52, 67–88.

Briefly, the two forms of consciousness, which can only be clearly distinguished in the abstract, are the receptive mode and the action mode. The action mode is one of logic, control, analysis, and prediction. It operates in a world of sign, concept, and system. It is a necessary function which, by its need to focus on explanation, limits the possibilities of our awareness—particularly in a secular world view. The receptive mode is one of association, surrender, intuition, and surprise. It operates in a world of symbol, ritual, and story. It is an often neglected function which, by diffusing our awareness, allows the possibility of new or expanded consciousness. It is a difficult form or sense of experience for a people socialized to think for control.

Arthur Deikmann, a psychologist, has developed the theory that the mystical experience—by which is meant simply the awareness of the presence of God (others speak of transcendental experiences, peak experiences, ecstasies, etc.)—becomes possible when we move out of the action mode of consciousness into the receptive mode. The action mode is necessary for theological reflection upon that experience, so to make this suggestion is not to deprecate the action mode. Rather it is only to describe what appears to occur in human consciousness in authentic prayer.

Deikmann calls this process *deautomization*. He has analyzed this phenomenon particularly in the methods of meditation. The term automization is derived from the fact that a society teaches us how to think. Our society values, predominantly if not exclusively, the action mode of consciousness. We think automatically in that mode, which makes prayer seem very "unnatural" for us. To pray effectively we need to get behind our socialization. Many spiritual images that will follow in this survey have just that purpose.

Another psychologist who has explored the nature of mystical experience, Ralph W. Hood, Jr., points out that persons capable of deeply sensible prayer are those whose religion seems to be intrinsic rather than extrinsic. These categories were first developed by Gordon Allport, a devout Episcopalian and one of the founders of humanistic psychology, to distinguish religious motivation. Intrinsic religion is characterized by health. Religious faith is a source of the growth and expansion of the horizons of our knowing. It enables risk. Extrinsic religion is defensive. It encourages the person to exclude others and may even breed a kind of paranoia, as exemplified in the mass suicides of the People's Temple in Guyana in November of 1978. Its greatest enemy is risk.

A number of references will be made throughout this study to pietism. Pietism is particularly characteristic of a spirituality that is found in extrinsic religious motivation. It is sentimental, rather than sensible. There is real fear, if not outright rejection, of mystical experience in pietism.

An Anthropology of Prayer

A parallel theory to bimodal consciousness comes from anthropology and has been developed particularly by Victor Turner (see *The Ritual Process*, Aldine Press, 1969). This theory is that human relationships fall into two types: 1) those defined by the structures with their roles and statuses; and 2) those lacking definition and existing within our common human condition. The first type of relationship is called the *structure* and the second type the *antistructure*.

The action mode of consciousness is highly valued in the structure among human institutions where order and predictability provide a sense of security. Authentic prayer—which is deeply sensible of God, who speaks out of the depths, and in an awareness of the chaos that surrounds us—requires that we move out of the structure into the antistructure. Here the receptive mode of consciousness is operative.

For this reason the wilderness or desert experience—translatable into such devotional practices as silent retreats, pilgrimages, times alone, etc.—has a.central place in the spiritual life of the Christian. It is also why there is, by necessity, much risk in the authentic life of prayer. The antistructure is inhabited by demons (those forces which destroy us) as well as by angels (the messengers of God). We will discover that in societies where there is little sense of self-worth this can be translated into a belief in the malevolent nature of the world, such as is identified in witchcraft.

A further observation of a general kind, related to the evolution of human consciousness, needs to be made. The history of Christian spirituality has come under severe criticism in recent years because of its stand on human sexuality. Clearly, for most of the time, our ascetical forebears were opposed to sexual activity of any kind and, as a result, many male spiritual masters were misogynists. While this attitude is not to be condoned today on either count, it is understandable from our past.

Someone has said that civilization advanced by conquering the Great Mother—i.e., the generic feminine deity, the earth mother, the fertility goddess—with the masculine forces of reason and analysis. In other words, human consciousness moved from the antistructure or receptive mode into the structure or action mode. This is undoubtedly true. It was a hard won victory and the "enemy"—symbolized by the feminine and by sexuality—remained a real threat. Humanity feared the chaos of living once again under the caprice of passion.

The price we paid for this "victory" was excessive, and through the centuries it took its toll. This survey, with its accounts of ritual castration, deprecation of marriage (if not of women themselves), and repression of orectic forces, will give ample evidence of a compulsive and forced masculine spirituality. The movement from the antistructure to the structure, from the receptive mode to the action mode of consciousness, was necessary and understandable, as much as the results are to be mourned. What we have to do now is reclaim the feminine spirituality and the place of sexuality—even genitality—in the life of prayer, without gainsaying the positive elements in our spiritual heritage drawn from the evolving human consciousness.

A Sociology of Prayer

One frontier of the study of Christian spirituality, for which little has been done to date, is the relationship between the shifting styles of spirituality—i.e., the dominance in turn of apophatic/speculative, speculative/kataphatic, kataphatic/affective, or affective/apophatic—and the nature of human institutions. The hypothesis is that a relation exists, just as it does in all forms of knowledge, and that this expresses itself in styles of devotional action characteristic of an age. Having stated the hypothesis, any documentation must be offered very hesitantly.

There are some tentative and partial correlations. Apophatic forms of prayer seem to be related to the collapse of social institutions. The fourth and fifth centuries and the fourteenth century were times of an emphasis on apophatic prayer. The decline of the Roman Empire and the shaking of the structures of feudalism, particularly as effected by the plague, coincide with these times. The early apophatic period was more speculative than the latter, perhaps because it coincided with a particularly fertile time of philosophical thought (Neo-Platonism), whereas the latter period, the fourteenth century, coincided with the decline of a fertile intellectual period, scholasticism, and the development of a particularly sterile period of philosophy, nominalism. (Scholasticism is the school of philosophical inquiry which lies behind our scientific method, and it grew out of the rediscovery in the West of Aristotle's work. Nominalism is a philosophical skepticism which implies that we cannot know anything in reality, because there is no real or true relationship between objects of our experience.)

Pietism, which can be defined briefly here as the confusion of subjective, superficial feelings with theology, follows a period of theological sterility: the fifteenth century following nominalism; the late seventeenth and eighteenth centuries folowing Protestant scholasticism; and today, following the radical or "death of God" theology of the 1960s. Since pietism is an exaggeration of a kataphatic/affective spirituality, it would be indicative of a time in which the environment provided rich imagery—e.g., the Renaissance or a later Baroque and Rococo artistic taste, as well as a nostalgia for the religion of the American frontier—without the corrective of a disciplined common intellectualism.

Occultism, particularly witchcraft, seems to accompany pietism. Mary Douglas, an anthropologist, has suggested that witchcraft flourishes in societies where there is a low sense of individual personal power and where roles are ill-defined. The external boundaries are very sharp, but one feels tyrannized by something "outside" oneself. The source of our affliction is identified with external malevolent forces.

The great text on sorcery, which became the principal reference book of the Inquisition, *Malleus Maleficarum,* was published in or about 1490. It was written by two Dominican priests, the same order which a century before produced the Rhineland mystics. This is the time in which the literature which had influence on the Protestant Reformation flourished. The Salem witch trials were in 1692. They were contemporary with fathers of that pietistic fervor that profoundly shaped American spirituality in persons like John Wesley, George Whitefield, and Jonathan Edwards.

What redeems the paranoid excesses of an affective piety is a speculative or thinking spirituality. Under what circumstances does this occur? It is interesting to ask, and an answer is not readily forthcoming. But there does seem to be the possibility of a corrective in situations where there is relative political predictability, which begets a fertile intellectual climate, and where the individual has some sense of self-worth. Illustrations would be Egypt in the third century (as contrasted with the Roman Empire in the West), the twelfth-century Renaissance, the sixteenth-century humanism, and the eighteenth and nineteenth centuries in Europe (but not in America). World wars, genocide, the horror of the bomb, and the loss of individual power, have called that sense of self-worth into question for us in the twentieth century.

The spirituality of Western Europe in the twelfth and thirteenth centuries was particularly sensible. It was less speculative and more affective, less apophatic and more kataphatic than the piety of that earlier "golden age" (the third, fourth, and fifth centuries) or of the East. Why? It may well have had something to do with the relatively stable sociopolitical climate, combined with the rich influx of new ideas. It was an exciting time, in which there was a freedom within limits and a new sense of order emerging out of relative chaos. One did not have to go into the desert to find God. The monasteries were in the middle of the city and a saint could be king of France—i.e., Louis IX (1214–1270; feast day August 25).

This is not intended to draw a naïve or idealistic picture or be anything more than suggestive. The belief is that what we do, even when we pray, is defined to a great extent by the sociocultural environment in which we live. The reader is invited to test his memory of history against the individuals and images found in this survey in hope that the correlation may become more accurate and clearer.

The Identification of Images

In each age, and often in each individual, the experience of God is thematized by certain key images. These images represent both the way to openness before God and the result of the experience of God. They may or may not have power for us. But there is value in knowing them, both for understanding the person in relation to the period in which he or she lived and for their possibilities for illumining our own experience today. Images will be identified with those persons and periods in which they are most characteristic.

In this analysis we will identify those images both by period and school, as well as by individual. More important, however, we will make a distinction between them as to whether they pertain to the training of the Christian pilgrim or to the goal. Ascetical theology traditionally defines the manner in which the Christian seeks to shape his life so that he might be open to the gift of God's salvific presence. Unless one holds that grace is given to some by "ramming it down their throats," and is denied others by God, there is always an ascetical theology in every school of Christian thought—implicit, if not explicit. We will speak of the images pertaining to ascetical theology as instrumental. Mystical theology traditionally describes the manner of humanity's union with God, which is one way of speaking of the goals of the life lived under grace. We will label images that seek to describe this as terminal. For convenience sake, both sets of images will be listed at the end of each section.

Issues in Spiritual Reading

The body of writing in the Christian spiritual tradition is large, even if we confine our search to those books in English that are readily available. It is easy to become lost in the materials and discouraged in our reading. There are a number of issues, however, which are pivotal in spiritual theology and provide a "handle" on the spiritual tradition as one reads. There are five issues suggested here.

1. It has been said that in every person there is a "God-shaped hole" waiting to be filled by God. In other words, humans are incomplete without God and have a built-in capacity for God. *What does that "hole" look like in a particular spiritual master?* The reader will find references to a "seed of reason" or a "spark of the soul," to the "inner eye" or "eye of love," as well as to the image of God within us. It would be helpful for those who wished to raise the theological question of the relationship of nature to grace in this light.

2. In the mid-1970s many cars in America sported a bumper sticker reading "We've found it." Apparently "it" referred to a saving relationship with Jesus Christ. If the author in question had a "bumper sticker" announcing that he or she had found "it," *what would "it" look like? What is the nature and possibility of the union between God and humanity? How does the author deal with the issue of transcendence versus immanence? Does the individual survive mystical union?*

3. In contemporary psychology, education, and theology we are very interested in the development of the individual. Erik Erikson has described eight stages of psychosexual development, Jean Piaget has discovered four stages of cognitive development, Lawrence Kohlberg has outlined six stages of moral development, and James Fowler has identified six stages of faith development. They all connote a process of maturation or coming to wholeness. *What is the process of development described in the work of a given Christian spiritual master? Or is there any? What is the place of ethical behavior in relation to spiritual maturation for him or her?*

4. A few years ago a survey was asking church people to describe someone who was "spiritually mature." The results, with some exceptions, were depressing. The answers largely reflected secular values, descriptive of someone who is effective in society. *How would a given Christian author describe the spiritually mature person?* Think about the issues of the relationship of body, emotions, mind, society, and soul—or spirit. Reflect on law and grace, works and faith.

5. As we shall see, it is totally erroneous to think that the Protestant Reformation "recovered the Bible" for Christians. The Scriptures are integral, almost without exception, to all ages and places of Christian spiritual reflection. It is also true that "literalism" is a modern heresy—perhaps the only heresy invented in modern times. *How does the Christian spiritual master interpret the Scriptures? What is the author's understanding of history in relation to the Scriptures?*

In order to assist the reader in consulting the primary sources themselves, a select bibliography will be found at the end of each section where it is appropriate and materials are available. Selections are based upon English editions which are, first, currently in print and, second, if not in print, available in a good theological library.

·I·

The Early Church

Jewish Antecedents

The spirituality of Judaism in the centuries prior to Christ was largely kataphatic and speculative. It was grounded in synagogal worship, which consisted principally of the reading and interpretation of the Hebrew Scriptures (our Old Testament) and the reciting of the prayers nourished by those Scriptures, particularly the blessing/thanksgiving (called the *Berakah*).

These images dominate: *d'ath* or knowledge (*hokmah* or wisdom), the *Shekinah* of Jewish mysticism, and *poverty*.

1. *D'ath* is the kind of knowing that is not just *about* something, but that takes possession of the person known. It is the knowledge which gives birth to confidence. It is to accept mystery, not deny it. It is to discern the designs of God. The Jewish sage—as in Proverbs, Job, Ecclesiastes, Ecclesiasticus, the Wisdom of Solomon, etc.—is one who possesses *d'ath* or *hokmah*. It comes from a lifetime of reading the Hebrew Scriptures, praying them, and reflecting upon them.

2. *Shekinah* means the dwelling of God with his people perceived, not in idols but as one would see the sun's rays coming from behind a dark cloud. It is the manifestation of God. It is the provisional presence of God, not the God present in the Day of Yahweh or at the consummation of all things. It is the presence of God in the Holy of Holies of the Temple or where two or three

14

meet to meditate upon the Torah, or where a righteous judge makes a decision. (The Torah at this time meant more than the first five books of the Old Testament. It also meant interpretation and tradition.) As the psalmist writes, "In thy light do we see light" (36:9). The notion of the *Shekinah* and *d'ath* is a theme that will recur in Christian mysticism as mystery and *gnōsis.*

The *Shekinah* is the presence of the holy in the midst of the profane. But the metaphor is that the *Shekinah* is like the sun; it is everywhere. Yahweh is present in the totality of his creation. He can appear in a burning bush as much as in the Holy of Holies. The *Shekinah* is particularly present in the charismatic person. While protecting the strict monotheism of Judaism, a parallel had to be noted between the Christian notion of the Holy Spirit and the "spirit of the *Shekinah."*

It is interesting that in the twelfth- and thirteenth-century *Kabbalah,* a Jewish mystical sect, the *Shekinah* becomes the feminine principle in the ten emanations of God, known as the *Sefiret.* This form of Judaism was directly influenced by Neo-Platonism, which shall be discussed later.

The idea of mystery in Judaism has its roots in the Persian and Greek influences upon the Jews during the intertestamental period. There is a fringe of rabbinical Judaism, known as the *ha-aminim,* who were concerned for mystery. The Essenes, a sect within Palestinian Judaism before and after the time of Jesus, were influenced by these Persian and Greek speculations. From the second century B.C., there were closed mystical sects within Judiasm. There also was an inner dynamic within the Pharisees toward mysticism. It has been argued that within the Diaspora there was a symbolic understanding of the Hebrew Scriptures, more like that of the Christians of the third century than of the Palestinian and Babylonian rabbinic tradition.

3. In the days of the patriarchs wealth was a sign of God's pleasure. This is not true of later Judaism. When there seems to be no reasonable hope in this world, an intentionally religious people may develop an apocalypticism: the belief that God is

breaking into the world to bring everything to a conclusion. It is often associated with the anticipation of Messiah and/or millennialism (i.e., the end of a thousand years). Apocalypticism is characteristic of oppressed people, the "have nots." Their expectations are not cluttered with the things of this world. The Jews under the Chaldeans, the Persians, the Seleucids, the Ptolomies, and the Romans—all before the time of Christ—were such an oppressed people. Poverty became an ascetical virtue. The psalmist says, "I know that the Lord maintains the cause of the afflicted, and executes justice for the needy" (140:12). The notion of poverty, sometimes in an exaggerated form, was to occur in Christianity as well.

One concluding note needs to be made. A Jewish Hellenistic philosopher, PHILO (c.20 B.C.–c.A.D. 50) will influence the Christian ascetical tradition particularly in two ways: First, he may well have been the father of both pagan and Christian mysticism in his theory that the Spirit of God takes the place in humanity of our spirit, as finds expression in the mind, or *nous;* Second, in his teaching that the allegorical method of biblical interpretation gives access to the hidden, true meaning of the Scriptures.

There will be frequent references to Philo as this study unfolds. His methods, as well as his categories, become a bridge, not only between the Hebrew Scriptures and the Hellenistic culture but also between Greek Christians and their Jewish roots. This is a time of apology, translation, and syncretism. There is no "pure strain" of any culture—Jewish, Greek, Persian, Roman—and the intellectual of the age sought to express his experience of God in such a way that he could identify, clarify, and share it so that it was understandable to the greatest number of people. Philo was a skillful and imaginative thinker and did just this preeminently.

Instrumental Images
   Poverty.
   Allegorical Method of Interpretation.

Terminal Images
  Shekinah.
  Wisdom.

New Testament

The people of the New Testament are, in the main, Jewish. The spirituality of the New Testament, particularly the Synoptics, is Jewish. It is kataphatic. Since it is not the religion of the Jewish intelligentsia, it is more affective than speculative.

In the Synoptics three images are introduced: *metanoia,* the desert, and purity of heart. Christian spirituality, building upon its Jewish roots—including *gnōsis* or wisdom, the *Shekinah,* and poverty—will develop these synoptic images.

Metanoia is translated as "repentance." "John the baptizer appeared in the wilderness, preaching a baptism of repentance (*metanoia*) for the forgiveness of sins" (Mk. 1:4). *Metanoia* means literally to change one's mind. It is related to *gnōsis* and will later be appropriated in a new way as the church builds on Philo's Hellenistic notion of the Spirit of God in the mind of humanity. Even here it does not mean just being sorry for your sins. It is to welcome the judgment of God and his transforming power into whatever we are—*and fundamentally we are what we think!*

The desert or wilderness, in both John the Baptist and Jesus as in the Old Testament, is a place of encounter. It is there that we wrestle with the demons and the angels, because that is where they are found—more so than in the city. This image has to do with poverty, not only poverty of material wealth but poverty as nakedness of spirit. "Blessed are the poor in spirit: for theirs is the kingdom of heaven" (Mt. 5:3).

Another image of poverty, which is related to the *Shekinah,* is purity of heart. "Blessed are the pure in heart: for they shall see God" (Mt. 5:8). Sören Kierkegaard defined purity of heart as the ability to will one thing. This relates it to *gnōsis* and *metanoia,* but also to a willingness to see in the light of God. Purity of heart and its promise of seeing God provide an archetypical image for Christian spirituality in all ages.

Paul is less affective than the Synoptics. The Middle Platonic notion that humankind is tripartite—composed of body, soul, and spirit—appears to be a commonplace assumption for him. It is presumptuous to compress Paul's spirituality into one or two images, but one or two such images can be suggestive of the complexity of his thought. Such a consideration can begin with the verse: "But we have the mind [*nous*] of Christ" (I Cor. 2:16). To this we can add verses such as: "And do not be conformed to this world: but be transformed by the renewing of your mind [*nous*]" (Romans 12:2); and "Be renewed in the spirit of your mind [*nous*]" (Eph. 4:23). Perhaps the best known statement by St. Paul of this kind is: "Have this mind among yourselves, which you have in Christ Jesus" (Phil. 2:5). The difference from the other verses lies in the use of the verb *phroneite* literally: "Think this [thing] in yourselves, which [thing] is in Christ Jesus."

In the Synoptics, thinking as Christ thinks is the same thing as repenting. The call to transformation by the renewal of our minds is what *metanoia* means. Like Philo, Paul holds that the union with God comes about as the Spirit of God—which sometimes appears to be confused with Christ—possesses the person. As one would expect in the first century, this is explained in terms of the mind. With this before us we can understand how Paul deals with the problem of humanity's fundamental sinfulness, as in Romans 7:21–8:5. In this passage Paul tells us that the law of sin wars against the law of the mind, but that when we have the mind of Christ we can overcome the lower self, where the law of sin rules. For those who say there is no mysticism, save possibly some eschatological expectation, in Paul this passage from Romans appears to be a clear refutation.

Let us not try to avoid as well the fact that there is a call to ascetical practice in Paul, which has inspired the church down through the centuries. "Work out your own salvation with fear and trembling" (Phil. 2:12). This is not a Pelagian admonition, but neither is it a testimony to the total depravity of man. For Paul the Christian is like an athlete—another image we need to remember— who constantly trains that he might win the prize: the appropriation of God's gift of himself revealed in Christ.

For Paul the image of the Cross is what opens the mind to the Spirit. "For the word of the cross is folly to those who are perishing, but to us who are being saved it is the power of God" (I Cor. 1:18). The Cross is the imaginative shock that blows the filters of humanity's awareness and opens us to the grace—i.e., the power and presence of God—that bestows upon us the mind of Christ.

What is it we have when we have the mind of Christ: "the mystery [to mustēoion] hidden for ages and generations and now made manifest to his saints" (Col. 1:26). This mystery is the great secret of God's plan for humanity, revealed in Jesus Christ. It is interesting that Paul has ambivalent feelings about gnōsis, knowledge, but occasionally it creeps in as a positive virtue. For example, in Colossians 2:3 he tells us that the love (agapē) of God will unite us in the knowledge (epignōsis and gnōsis) of the mystery.

For the fourth gospel is kataphatic, but perhaps a bit more affective than Paul, yet not as much as the Synoptics. The predominant image here is *light versus darkness.* The glory (doxa), which is the *Shekinah,* the veiled evidence of God's presence, is the light. Light is life. "In him was life, and the life was the light of men. The light shines in the darkness, and the darkness has not overcome it. . . . We have beheld his glory, glory as the only Son from the Father" (Jn. 1:4–5, 14).

As in Paul, the Cross is an important image, but not so much an imaginative shock as it is an image of glory. The Evangelist plays on the Greek word *airein,* by which he obviously implies both lifting up on the Cross and lifting up to exalt. There is not so much scandal here as in Paul.

Furthermore, the goal of the spiritual life is not *gnōsis* but *agapē* (love). It is not an affective, emotional love, however. It is the love exemplified in the Cross, the washing of feet, and the caring for the unlovable. One thing we will discover is the way in which knowledge and love vary in importance as the manifestation of the presence of God in the person open to his grace. In the third, fourth, and fifth centuries knowledge will prevail, in the eleventh through the fourteenth love will take over.

The centrality of the image of love in the fourth gospel is perhaps surprising, since the Evangelist begins with a discussion of logos, clearly evoking thoughts of the Stoic principle of the unifying reason (i.e. Logos), which pervades the cosmos. Logos (reason) and *sōphia* (wisdom) are both related to *gnōsis*. In the Stoic anthropology every person has a seed of reason, *Logos spermatikos,* which image both describes humanity as possessing a potentiality for union with the divine—i.e., humanity as spirit—and suggesting the purpose of an ascetical discipline: the cultivation of that seed. The Evangelist does not follow this line of argument, but subsequent spiritual masters shall.

Instrumental Images	*Terminal Images*
Metanoia.	Mind of Christ.
Christian athlete.	Light.
Cross.	Love (*agapē*).
Purity of heart.	Logos.

The Apostolic Fathers

The writings of the post-New Testament authors tend to be naïve until the sophisticated discourse of Irenaeus of Lyon. They have a kataphatic yet moderately speculative bent.

The gift of *gnōsis* is a dominating image, although the second century struggled with the heretical Gnostics. Therefore it is necessary to define carefully what is meant by knowledge. We have to keep in mind that this period lives in the disappointment of the apocalyptic expectations of both the Jews, as in the insurrection against Rome of A.D. 70 and A.D. 135, and the Christians, who expected the *Parousia* and got the church. Gnosticism as an heretical doctrine was an ahistorical dualism, based upon a meta-physic in which the world was divided among spirit, soul, and matter, exemplified in three distinct kinds of people. The even-tual evolution of Christian gnosticism is an historical dualism, in which the victory of God—creator, redeemer, and sanctifier—over the powers of evil is resolved in the possibility of the knowl-edge of God for all humankind.

The Epistle of Barnabas, the author tells us, is written that our knowledge may be perfected. Such knowledge is, however, a gift of God. If someone has it, the unforgivable sin is to turn away into darkness. Knowledge and light are synonymous. "The way of light is this: if someone is willing to journey on the way to the appointed place, let him make haste with his works. Therefore the knowledge [gnōsis] that has been given to us [is] to walk about in this sort of way" (Barnabas 19:1). Then follows a series of commandments, which includes a demand that one be simple in heart and full of the Spirit.

Simplicity of heart, aplotes, is the same thing as purity of heart, which is a great concern of the Apostolic Fathers. This biblical image should be kept clearly in mind, and we need to recall its relation to poverty. The opposite of purity of heart is double-mindedness (dipsychia). Double-mindedness particularly horrifies the Shepherd of Hermas. "Consider this double-mindedness: for it is wicked and foolish, and uproots many from faith; yes, even those who are very faithful and strong." Double-mindedness is to serve both God and mammon. In a world where martyrdom was a distinct possibility, one can understand how important it was only to live to be given the gift of the knowledge of God.

Encratism comes out of a pursuit of poverty carried to a logical absurdity, a kind of "quietism with a vengeance." Excessive zeal for purity of heart leads to *encratism*. The word is Greek, meaning self-controlled or disciplined. Polycarp, in his letter to the Phi-lippians, for example, says that deacons are to be "temperate [egkrateis] in all things" (Phil. 5:1). But temperance is "in the eye of the beholder." TATIAN, claimed by some to be the "father" of encratism, a gnostic heresy, despised all Greek culture, rejected matrimony as a form of adultery, and condemned both the use of meat in any form and the drinking of wine. One of the practices of the encratites was self-castration, celebrated corporately on occasion by running through the city streets holding one's testicles aloft. A Puritanism untempered by reason and suspicious of positive feelings is always in danger of encratism.

Of course, the most extreme expression of encratism was martyrdom. The word literally means to witness, and came to identify witness by death. IGNATIUS OF ANTIOCH (Feast day: October 17) wrote to the Romans, living in the city to which he was being brought to suffer death, "Suffer me to be eaten by the beasts, through whom I can attain to God" (Rom. 4:1). This is as clear an expression of ascetical practice as one can find! A whole theology of martyrdom developed around this experience. While it has roots in Judaism (cf. II Maccabees 6:7–7:41), martyrdom was related to baptism and the Eucharist, and the church was very ambivalent about those who openly sought martyrdom.

The imitation of Christ relates most directly to the wish to be assimilated to Christ. IRENAEUS (Feast day: June 28) countered the gnostic heresies by arguing for an understanding of Christ grounded in Paul's speculations of Christ as the "second Adam" (I. Cor. 15:45) and the Logos christology of the fourth gospel. This is called *recapitulation.* What we lost by the sin of the first Adam we have regained and then some by our identification with the Christ, centering in his Passion. The true *gnosis* is the Logos of Christ, which illumines the free will of humanity, enabling it to conquer sin and death and become like God.

Instrumental Images

    Purity of heart, simplicity (*aplōtes*) as opposed
       to double-mindedness (*dipsychia*).
    Temperance, of which the exaggeration is encratism.
    Martyrdom.

Terminal Images
   Knowledge/light.
   Recapitulation.

SELECT BIBLIOGRAPHY
Apostolic Fathers: New Translations of Early Christian Writings,
   edited by Jack Sparks. Nelson, 1978.
Irenaeus, *Excerpts from the Works,* edited by Roberts, Alexander,
   and Robinson. St. Charles House, 1973.

Alexandrian School

Before we consider the Alexandrian Christian spiritual masters, who are so central to the development of spiritual theology in the church, it is necessary that two phenomena be described briefly: the hermetic literature and the rise of Neo-Platonism.

The hermetic books, consisting of eighteen treatises dealing largely with occult subjects (magic, astrology, alchemy, etc.), were attributed to Hermes Trismegistus—literally "Hermes the thrice-great"—the Egyptian god Thoth, or to Poimandres, the "shepherd of men." They are a syncretistic collection, typical of the mystical writings of that period, and related to the Old Testament in the tradition of Philo. The most interesting is the first treatise or book, the Poimandres. Here the writer tells us that we must strip away the physical world·to discover the intelligible world. At the source of all is mind, who creates another mind, which in turn creates fire, spirit, and the seven angels. The seven angels rule the astral spheres through which the soul ascends to the knowledge of God, which is participation in the absolute mind and is the same as salvation.

Neo-Platonism is a philosophy with overtones of a religion. Its beginnings are found in the teaching of Ammonius Saccas, but claims as its formative father, Plotinus, a pupil of Ammonius. Plotinus was an Alexandrian who ended up teaching in Rome. Absolute transcendence is for Plotinus the One who is totally other. There are two other hypostases or manifestations of the transcendent: Mind and Soul. Creation is a procession or emanation from the One. Soul has two parts, as does humanity, which comes from the World-soul: these two parts are rational and irrational soul. Plotinus is not always clear about the nature of the soul. Sometimes it has three parts: the rational, the spirited, and the appetitive. The irrational or appetitive is related to matter or the body. It is more important to keep in mind that Plotinus did not teach a dualistic philosophy but was really a monist.

The salvation of humanity is the result of the purification of the mind or rational soul by an ascent through the emanations of the One to participation in the divine Mind. As there is a procession from the One, so is there a return to the One. These spheres are a very important image, as we shall see throughout the thousand years that followed. The ascent is twofold: a prior intellectual ascent, known in Greek as *theoria;* and a logically subsequent ascent, known in Greek as *praxis.* The relation of *theoria* and *praxis* is still discussed in Marxist philosophy today, as well as in pastoral and moral theology. The motivation of the ascent is *eros* or natural love, the urge for unity with the One.

In the ascent, Plotinus teaches, there are four movements: purgation and the practice of the virtues, a rising above sense perception to thought, a reaching beyond thought to union, and an ecstatic absorbtion in the One. We will discover that the first three movements become fundamental to Christian spirituality, as do many of the concepts defined by Plotinus, drawing on the religious and philosophical speculation that went before him.

The Alexandrian Christian spiritual masters developed their thought parallel to and in the same intellectual climate as the hermetic books and Neo-Platonism. It is inevitable that certain common images and concepts emerge, which, because of the centrality of Alexandria in the philosophical and theological world, left its mark on Christian spiritual theology to this very day.

Whereas there is no formal "school" in Alexandria in the third century, this period and center is represented by two significant persons: CLEMENT OF ALEXANDRIA (Feast day: December 5) and Origen. They both are kataphatic and highly speculative. Their thought develops together with a secular philosophy, Neo-Platonism, which is as much Stoic as Platonic, with highly metaphysical overtones from various Near Eastern religious thought. It is difficult to exaggerate both the influence of Neo-Platonism upon Christian thinking, even up to the present, and, at the same time, the clear differences between the unabridged form of Neo-Platonism and the Gospel of Jesus Christ interpreted by those trained in Neo-Platonic thought.

Two images stand out in Clement. The first is *gnōsis,* the gift of the Logos, the Christ. *Gnōsis* is not something we finally achieve, although Clement vigorously defends the importance of what we would call the "secular disciplines" (e.g., philosophy). Clement is the prototypical Christian humanist, but ultimately *gnōsis* is the gift of God. It is the illumination of our minds and, therefore, of ourselves—since for Clement the true self is the rational self. *Gnōsis* leads us not only to the apprehension of intelligible realities, but beyond those to the hidden meaning of the spiritual realities. The created order is a symbol of such realities, particularly the Scriptures.

One encratic principle which continues to gain momentum is the ascetical practice of avoiding sexual intercourse. Virginity will become an ideal. This is related to the understanding of the supreme characteristic of humanity: reason. Reason is in the head or brain and it is masculine. Therefore, women, while in orthodox Christianity are clearly considered fully human, are less given to reason, and contact with them leads out of reason. There is a vivid description in Clement's writings of how intercourse causes the blood to rush from the head to the penis thereby rendering us less than human. While one may not agree with this description of what it is to be human—to be reasonable and that alone— granting that premise and the Logos christology that builds upon it, the prohibition against sexual intercourse and the warnings about women are understandable. (One curious result of this fear of the feminine is that it closes Christian spirituality to one—and perhaps the most natural—entry to the receptive mode of consciousness: the identification of the feminine in each of us.)

The second image which Clement introduces arises from this concern: *apatheia*. The Greek word for passion is *pathē*. The alpha at the beginning is something like "un-," making this literally "unpassion." It does not mean, however, apathy (which is the English derivative), nor does it mean a complete suppression of feeling. Remember that God, to a Greek, is without passion or emotion (i.e., impassible), and so to be related to God one must expect the calming of our disordered passions. God gives us his love, so *apatheia* is not the absence of love but the absorption into the truth that is love. But it is thoroughly reasonable love!

ORIGEN was less serene, more tortured, than Clement. He is not a "disciple" of Clement, but was probably taught by Ammonius Saccas (c.175–242), the "father behind the father [Plotinus]" of Neo-Platonism. There is little question but that Origen is the seminal thinker in the history of Christian spirituality, particularly in the East. Origen was an encratite in his youth. He was reported by some biographers to have castrated himself. He never lost his love for austere discipline. Origen says, "Nothing that is seen is good." He has to modify this in the face of the sacraments; but one gets the feeling he does so reluctantly.

The Cross for him, despite his brilliance and profound learning, is the heart of the matter—and the Cross is a symbol of conflict. It is the centrality of the Cross which gives to Origen's understanding of *gnōsis* a sophistication Clement does not possess. Everything for him is struggle and temptation.

Origen's asceticism is dominated by several images. The reflective reading of the Scriptures, using an allegorical method, leads to the knowledge of spiritual realities. All things in the open are related to things hidden, and the trick is to find the path from the former to the latter. The centrality of the Scriptures is true of all the great Christian spiritual masters and is not an idea generated in the Protestant Reformation. Origen stands in the tradition of the Jewish *haggada,* as do countless Christian commentators upon the Bible. (The *haggada* are the non-prescriptive expansions on the Hebrew Scriptures, such as legends, folk tales, homilies, etc.). Origen was very biblical, but not very historical.

The Christian ascetic, as Origen sees it, seeks to imitate and participate in Christ. The spiritual life is a process of progressive detachment from the world. To imitate Christ is to live the Cross, which leads to illumination by the Logos. Not everyone can do that, which results in a kind of "practical gnosticism" in Origen's approach.

This process of illumination begins with self-knowledge. Philo claimed the Greeks got this idea from Solomon, but it dominates Origen's thinking and practically every Christian spiritual master that followed him. There are two kinds of self-knowledge. One demands a constant struggle with demons, against which the Cross is the supreme expression and hope. The other is a gift of God. It comes with "sober intoxication"—another kind that appears in Philo and later in Gregory of Nyssa. Origen developed an allegorical exposition of the life of Moses as typical of the growth in holiness which Gregory of Nyssa will later amplify. We are always wanderers, "always on the road and under canvas."

It is with the image of spiritual combat that third-century men and women understood the need to go out into the desert to fight the demons and to find the angels. Both the demons and the angels were believed to live there in the desert. (Never make the naïve mistake of secular Christianity by thinking they went into the desert to "escape!")

It is interesting to see how Origen teaches the Neo-Platonic concept of the double ascent of the soul to God: *theoria* and *praxis.* He reminds us that the Scriptures tell us that Moses and Aaron led the Israelites through the wilderness by their hand— i.e., two hands. The one hand is *theoria,* the ascent of the intellect; the other hand is *praxis,* the ascent of virtue. Like almost all the ancient spiritual masters, Origen believed that the purity of the soul is manifested in the love of one's neighbor or in goodness.

Origen in his *Commentary*, as well as in his *Homilies on the Canticle* describes the marriage of the soul and the Logos. (The Song of Songs provides a favorite source of material for the Christian spiritual masters through the centuries.) Such a marriage opens us to the deepest mystery, and becomes the heart of Origen's mystical theology. We are to be as much like God as possible. Union with the Logos blossoms forth into union with God. Prayer ascends to the Father through the Son. The goal is *aporata stasis*, the restoration of all things in God (cf. Acts 3:21).

A critical question in the history of mystical theology is whether the "advanced Christian" achieves union, even absorption, with the Logos; that is: Do we ever "arrive"? Origen may imply that he does—something which Gregory of Nyssa refutes a century later. This passage from the *First Homily on the Canticle* is both a personal testimony to his struggle and an implication that the struggle is momentarily resolved in God.

> The Bride [the church] then beholds the Bridegroom [the Word]; and He, as soon as she has seen Him, goes away. He does this frequently throughout the Song; and that is something nobody can understand who has not suffered it himself. God is my witness that I have often perceived the Bridegroom drawing near me and being most intensely present with me; then suddenly He has withdrawn and I could not find Him; though I sought to do so. I long for Him to come again, and sometimes He does so. Then, when he has appeared and I lay hold of Him, He slips away once more; and, when He has so slipped away, my search for Him begins anew. So does he act with me repeatedly, until in truth I hold Him and go up, 'leaning on my Nephew's arm.'

There is a timeless quality to this very personal testimony of a holy man who died over 1700 years ago. He is the font of most ideas in Christian spirituality.

Instrumental Images
   Apatheia, particularly virginity.
   Reflective reading of the Scriptures to discern hidden meaning.
   Spiritual combat with demons.

Terminal Images
   Gnōsis, the knowledge of spiritual realities behind intelligibles.
   Marriage of the soul with the *Logos.*

SELECT BIBLIOGRAPHY
Alexandrian Christianity: Selected Translations of Clement and Origen,
   edited by John Ernest, Leonard Oulton, and Henry Chadwick.
   (Library of Christian Classics, Vol. 2) Westminister Press,
   1954.
——, *The Song of Songs: Commentary and Homilies,* translated by
   Robert R. Lawson. (Ancient Christian Writers, Vol. 26).
   Paulist Press, 1957.

Monasticism

An alternative to martyrdom in the church became the precarious
life in the desert: *anchoritism.* It comes from the Greek, meaning
"to withdraw." People literally went into the desert to avoid martyrdom, but the severe life there was considered a worthy substitute for the final witness. There, as we have already indicated,
one fought the demons and found the angels. They were not necessarily of the intelligentsia. Their spirituality was often kataphatic and affective, unlike the more learned persons such as
Origen, whose writings survive.

Suffering was part of being an anchorite, but not the purpose.
Liberation or disengagement, in order to awaken the spirit to the
Word of God, was the purpose. This makes good sense if we
believe that to be human is to be rational and to be rational one
must avoid passion—as the intellectual world of the third and
fourth centuries believed. It was a life of continual meditation

upon Scriptures and a time of strenuous training in order that one might ascend the ladder of perfection by the grace of God. Monastics were not "trying to pull themselves up by their own bootstraps," but sought to quiet the inner self in order to hear the Word of God. (What Don Juan tells Carlos Castaneda to do in "stopping the world" in his contemporary description of his apprenticeship to a Yaqui Indian shaman.)

There were two forms of anchorite life: eremitical, which is life totally in solitude; and cenobitical, where the participants gathered in community from time to time each day.

The most oppressive demon to be fought in the desert, according to Evagrius Ponticus (d. 399) was *acedia* or "the devil of the noonday sun." It always remains the enemy of the spiritual life. The term comes from the Greek word *kedia* ("care,") with the alpha privative on front to make it "un-caring." Acedia is boredom, apathy, listlessness, or uncaringness. It is the inability to train and to remain disciplined because we no longer care, we have lost our intentionality and we give ourselves over to our feelings.

The image of the *ladder*—we get the word "climax" from the Greek word for ladder—occurs in religion for thousands of years. Little ladders were buried in Egyptian tombs to help the dead climb to the upper world. Jacob had a vision of a ladder between heaven and earth, with the angels ascending and descending upon it (Gen. 28:12). Plato and Philo speak of ladders, as do the Church Fathers after the third century (e.g., Gregory of Nyssa). It is a common image to the Desert Fathers, and will be an organizing principle for writings on spirituality from then until the present day. (Later we will write of John Climacus—i.e., John of the Ladder—and of Walter Hilton, author of the *Scale of Perfection, The Ladder of Perfection*.)

The image of the ladder gained impetus from the popular pagan Roman piety, which held that a soul upon death ascended through the spheres of heaven—the source of Paul's reference to "the third heaven" (II Cor. 12:2)—through a process of continued cleansing. Some of the pagan epitaphs from Roman tombs of the second and third centuries, reflecting the hope of the astral assent, are profoundly moving. The astral ascent was taken over in the cosmology of the Neo-Platonists and, as we shall see, was used by Dionysius the pseudo-Areopagite. Of course, we all know the ladder image well from Dante's *Divine Comedy*. But the purpose of going into the desert is to ascend the ladder of perfection, and what drags us down are all those distractions, culminating in *acedia*.

Instrumental Images
  Anchoritism.
  Combat against *acedia*.
  The ladder of perfection.

The Cappadocians

The fourth-century greats—Gregory of Nazianzen; Basil of Caeserea; and Basil's brother, Gregory of Nyssa—are described by Louis Bouyer as typifying "erudite monasticism." Basil was a legislator; Gregory Nazianzen, Basil's close personal friend, a poet; but Gregory of Nyssa was the spiritual master. We shall devote ourselves to GREGORY OF NYSSA (Feast day: March 9), whose spirituality tended toward the apophatic and speculative.

Gregory is the link between Philo and Origen and Dionysius the pseudo-Areopagite, Byzantine mysticism, and much of the apophatic tradition of the medieval church. He is sometimes known as the "father of Christian mysticism." He is a rationalist of the first order. To be irrational is to be like the beasts. Despite the fact that he himself was once married, he firmly adheres to *apatheia*. He particularly advocates virginity. Marriage is for Gregory a "sad tragedy," "a bodily union that works to produce a dead body." Physical virginity is only the shell for an inner virginity, which purifies the soul, makes it like the Spirit, and therefore open for a bond (*syndesmos*) with God.

But a caution is in order about too simple an interpretation of

Gregory's attitude toward marriage and that of others of the ancient church Fathers. We need to keep in mind that ancient man—and the word "man" is used advisedly—viewed romantic love as a disease. This was true of Christian and pagan alike. It is not until the twelfth-century "courts of love" that a contrary understanding arises. Furthermore, marriage and mating were not considered the same thing. Marriage was a social institution that existed to rear citizens of the state. There was little, if any, romantic glow around marriage, and mating was often viewed as an irrational indulgence. Women could, however, be highly admired and respected. Certainly Gregory held his mother and sister in high esteem, and there were some very powerful women in the early church. The very different corporate reality of the fourth-century person must not allow us to come to simplistic conclusions about what they thought or believed.

Gregory teaches that man has a proclivity for God (called after Paul in Phil. 3:11, *epectasy*), just as Philo and many of the Church Fathers such as Origen. This proclivity (what Karl Rahner calls "obediential potency") is what he understands to be the image of God in humanity. It pertains to the soul; but it is not just the mind (*nous*), as in the Alexandrians, or free will (*autezousion*), as in Irenaeus. It is the goodness or virtue (*aretē*) of God that finds a place in the goodness of man. It is no surprise, therefore, that Gregory is very concerned for the virtuous life.

Gregory believes that man is driven, and the inward drive is *eros:* love for oneness, which is only corrupted if it gives way to passion for pleasure. There are two marriages to which *eros* can lead us: the marriage of the flesh and the marriage of the spirit. The latter gives us the wisdom of God. One cannot have *two* marriages. To do so is to deny the purity of heart.

The spiritual life for Gregory is perpetual ascent. It begins in light and moves into the darkness. For the first time the image of darkness takes on real meaning. God is utterly ineffable and so is present in the darkness of humanity's mind. One is carried along by *eros,* which, when joined by the *agapē* (i.e., the love) of God, produces a "sober inebriation" (*nēphalios methē*), a term he gets from Origen and Philo. But one never "arrives." For the perfection of human nature consists perhaps in its very growth in goodness. "This is the true knowledge of what is sought: this is the seeing that consists in not seeing." One strives for the goal or mark (*skopos*)—the word "scope" comes from this: that to which we look. (It is interesting that the Greek word for "sin" means "the missing of the mark" or "missing that to which we look.")

But in the midst of the darkness there is a knowing of God (*theognosia*). God gives the soul an "intelligible light" (*neoton*), which is described as darkness. It is the presence of God that comes to the purified soul in its emptiness—seemingly a negative notion. It is the love of God that penetrates the soul that the soul might participate in God, which participation Gregory insists involves knowledge. He calls it a "compenetration." Gregory writes in the *Sixth Homily on the Canticle,* "This [peak of the soul's desire] having happened, the two [soul and God] emigrate [*metachorei:* change place, depart, etc.] into one another: for God comes to be in the soul and in turn the soul dwells together [*metoikizetai*] in God."

Does humanity have an immediate experience of the essence or existence of God? Gregory answers paradoxically: yes and no. The "yes" is contained in that word: *metachorei.* Perhaps it is a change of intuitive grasping—the Greek verbal root *chōreō* means to "reach" or "grasp"—of a divine apprehension, in which the subject that lies beyond the phenomena or appearances is given to our intuition.

The compenetration of God and man is a form of *synergy*—a concept which bothers Protestant theologians. The *eros* of humanity is, in this concept, redirected by the *agapē* of God and drawn into union with him. It is not a concept which argues that humanity reaches God by its own power, but that humankind has a natural longing for God that is fulfilled by God's presence. The word synergy comes from the Greek verb, meaning "to work together." Protestant theologians sometimes argue that *synergy* is a concept which denies that humanity is saved only by grace through faith. This does not have to be our understanding. The word appears in Paul's letter to the Romans: "We know that in everything God works [*synegei*—a better translation would be "works together"* for good with those who love him" (Romans 8:28). Here the concept seems to be very biblical.

The possibility of compenetration or emigration depends upon the awakening of the soul and the engendering of an inner quiet or peace by God's grace. In the history of Christian spirituality this is called *hesychia* or hesychasm. It is a concept common to all three of the Cappadocians and comes to play an absolutely crucial role in Eastern mysticism.

The result of compenetration raises the possibility of deification or divinization (*theopoieis* or *theosis*). The Greek words first appear in Clement of Alexandria. This is not to *become* God, but to *become like* God by virtue of God's adoption of us in the power of the Incarnation (including the Cross). For the Eastern church it is the "flip side" of the Incarnation. The Alexandrians allude to this, Athanasius mentions it, and Gregory of Nyssa affirms it. It becomes a firm mystical image in Eastern spirituality, however, beginning with Dionysius the pseudo-Areopagite.

Instrumental Images
 Epectasy.
 Eros.
 Sober inebriation.
 Hesychasm.
 Synergy.

Terminal Images
 Skopos.
 Compenetration or *metachōria.*

SELECT BIBLIOGRAPHY

Gregory of Nyssa, *Ascetical Works,* translated by Virginia Woods
   Callahan. (Fathers of the Church) Catholic University Press,
   n.d.

———*From Glory to Glory,* translated and edited by Henry Mu-
   surillo. Scribner's, 1961.

———, *The Life of Moses,* translated by Abraham J. Malherbe.
   Paulist Press, 1978.

Monasticism Again

An extended note about post-Cappadocian Eastern monasticism,
influenced by Gregory of Nyssa, is now in order. It becomes even
more apophatic and speculative to the point of abstraction.

A fascinating person, claiming to be Macarius—called the
PSEUDO-MACARIUS—a third-century anchorite, suggests two important images. The first is a terminal image. The mystical experience is for him one of *light.* We are not sure what he meant by
light, except that he says the "whole soul has become a spiritual
eye and entirely light." This builds on an earlier image. It also
plays heavily on the place of the heart in the life of prayer, which
will be developed in Byzantine spiritually in the fourteenth century.

The instrumental image describes the chief work of the anchorite: *constant prayer.* Such prayer does not lose itself in speaking, but concentrates on the name of Jesus. Here is a hint point-
ing to *monologistic prayer*—literally "one word or thought" prayer.
It calls to mind, maybe for the first time, the Jesus Prayer.

The Jesus Prayer may originally have been an Egyptian
apophthegm (i.e., "inspired utterance"): "Lord Jesus Christ, Son
of God, have mercy on me." The first explicit reference to the
Jesus Prayer we have is in the life of Abba Philemon, an Egyptian
hermit. The writing dates from the sixth or seventh century—
perhaps the early sixth century. Both Diadochos of Photike and
Neilos of Ancyra in the fifth century refer to the "remembrance"

of the Name of Jesus, but they do not mention the form. Fourth-century monastics mention other forms of monologistic prayer but not the Jesus Prayer. The idea goes back to the New Testament and the invocation of the Name (I Cor. 6:11, 12:3; Phil. 2:10). In fact, Paul says "I would rather speak five words with my mind, in order to instruct others, then ten thousand words in a tongue" (I Cor. 14:19). In Greek and Russian the Jesus Prayer is five words!

One last and important word about the pseudo-Macarius. He interpreted the images of purity of heart and *dipsychia* to say that sin and grace coexist in humanity. This marks him historically as a Messalian—a monastic sect which taught that united to every soul is a demon, which is defeated only by constant prayer. The sect was condemned by the third ecumenical council (431). (Some argue that Messalianism was condemned for social and economic reasons.) The writings of the pseudo-Macarius profoundly influenced the Hesychasts, but also John Wesley. What the pseudo-Macarius was saying is that humanity is at the same time sinner and justified, *simul peccator et justus*. The notion is not original with Luther.

The metaphor which Macarius in his homilies to the monks uses to describe humanity as justified and sinner at the same time is a charmingly picturesque window into his culture. There is, he says, a chariot race going on in the heart of every one of us between two charioteers. One is *nous*, the mind, driving with the reins of reason. The other is the chariot of Satan. He does not tell us who is driving the Devil's chariot, but Satan and the Holy Spirit are spectators, cheering on their respective champions.

Another significant person, whom we have already mentioned, is EVAGRIUS PONTICUS (346–399) a friend of the Cappadocians. He has come to be seen, to quote Bouyer, as "one of the most important names in the history of spirituality." Condemned by the fifth ecumenical council as an Origenist—he was a very enthusiastic follower of Origen—he made a lasting impact on Western spirituality prior to that condemnation, and he was a particular influence on John Cassian. Von Balthasar accuses him, however, of being more Buddhist than Christian. This is because Evagrius is an extreme advocate of apophatic prayer. Based upon the tripartite nature of humanity—body, soul, and spirit (including *nous*)—he taught three stages of spiritual progress: practice ending in *apatheia,* knowledge of divine reason, and knowledge of the Trinity. These three stages will find later far-reaching development. In the East they will become the prayer of the lips, the mind, and the heart. In the West, they become the purgative, the illuminative, and the unitative ways.

Evagrius is a very coherent and systematic author. He has a strong sense of demons. He identifies eight basic sins—ancestors of our seven capital sins: gluttony, luxury, love of money, sadness, anger, acedia, vainglory, and pride. One begins to fight demons with faith, followed by fear, continence, patience, and then hope. This begets *apatheia,* which is freedom from the dominance of the passions in order that love may be engendered. To pray without distraction is to have *apatheia.*

Perhaps most striking is Evagrius' notion of the knowledge of God. Unlike the pseudo-Macarius, he puts more emphasis on the mind (*nous*). Toward the last few centuries of the Byzantine Empire, Athonite spirituality will overthrow this emphasis, as will medieval Western piety. It is *knowledge* that God gives to the naked mind. Evagrius writes: "Blessed is he who has arrived at infinite ignorance [*agnosia*]." The contemplation of the Scriptures is not for Evagrius. It is the emptying of the mind. This becomes the inspiration for the Eastern teaching that two things stand in the way of the knowledge of God: passion and imagination.

Finally, to leap forward 250 years, one needs to make note of two spiritual masters. First, JOHN CLIMACUS (c.570–649), John of the Ladder of Paradise, after the name of his treatise using the image of the ladder. It has thirty "rungs," in accordance with the years of Jesus' life, and makes the imitation of our Lord the central instrumental image. There are those who have suggested that there are parallels between John Climacus' thirty steps to knowledge and the individuation process of C. G. Jung. John Climacus was very much an echo of Evagrius, although he had also read widely in other authors. His influence, through Simon, the New Testament theologian, on the Hesychasts in the fourteenth century is particularly notable in step 27 on solitude. It is the Byzantine Hesychasts who represent the golden age of the prayer of the heart, to which we shall be referring from time to time.

Second, ISAAC OF NINEVEH (died c.700) is an interesting figure. Clearly a descendent of Philo, Dionysius, and Evagrius; he also is an influential person for sufism, a form of Muslim mysticism. Isaac is an articulate spokesman for the necessity of tears (*penthos*) in the spiritual life—something those of us brought up in the belief that the Spirit always "leaves us laughing" need to know. He says: "So long as you have not reached the realm of tears, that which is hidden within you still serves the world— that is, you still lead a worldly life and do the work of God only with your outer man, while the inner man is barren; for his fruit begins with tears" (*Directions on Spiritual Tracing*, 219).

Instrumental Images
> Constant prayer.
> Monologistic prayer.
> Jesus Prayer.
> Coexistence of sin and grace.
> Identification of sins.
> Infinite ignorance or the naked mind.
> Tears or *penthos*.

Terminal Images
> Light.
> Knowledge of the Trinity.

SELECT BIBLIOGRAPHY
Evagrius Ponticus, *The Praktikos: Chapters on Prayer*, translated by John Eudes Bamberger. Cistercian Publications, 1972.

Isaac of Ninevah, *Mystic Treatises,* translated by A. J. Wensinck.
   Sandig, 1969.
John Climacus, *The Ladder of Divine Ascent,* translated by Lazarus
   Moore. Faber and Faber, 1959.

Dionysius the Pseudo-Areopagite

Eastern mysticism comes to a climax, and in a certain sense
an end, in the unknown author who claimed to be a certain
DIONYSIUS (the medieval church called him "Denis"). He it was
who heard Paul preach in Athens on the Hill of Ares, the Greek
god of war (Acts 17:22). His influence, curiously enough, is
probably greater in the Western church than in his native East.

   Whoever he was, he probably lived in the early fifth century,
possibly as a Syrian anchorite. He is speculative and apophatic.
Dionysius is an interesting mixture of a committed Christian,
grounded in the Scriptures and liturgy, using Neo-Platonic concepts to explain humanity's ascent by God's grace to his presence.

   Generally Dionysius teaches in the same tradition as Evagrius
and Gregory of Nyssa and is in the line of Alexandrian spirituality. There are three images which are particularly important to
him.

   The first is *hierarchy*. The cosmos is divided into nine spheres,
which do not so much separate the created order from God as
they express God's rule over all creation and the process whereby
one moves to achieve a sense of oneness with God. Such oneness
is the goal of humanity. Humankind's desire for God is *eros,*
which drives humanity upward in a Christian version of the astral
ascent. *Eros* is, however, renascent *agapē,* God's love for us manifest in the Logos. What Dionysius did was use the concepts of the
Neo-Platonic philosopher, Procus, to clarify the Christian experience. Hymn 599 in *The Hymnal 1940,* is straight Dionysius.

   The second image is *mystery*. Prior to Dionysius, "mystery" (as
in Paul) is God's hidden plan of salvation revealed in Christ, or a
synonym for "spiritual." Now Dionysius makes the mystical
things the object of the Scriptures and the end of our quest. He

builds on Gregory of Nyssa and Evagrius to argue that the mystery of God is found in the cloud and the darkness. The knowledge of God is in no way a result of the intelligible realities. Here he differs dramatically from Clement of Alexandria and Origen. It is the luminosity given by God which is the mystery. Unknowing lies at the heart of this experience. Kataphatic theology must be balanced by apophatic theology.

The third image we have already mentioned, but it gets explicit treatment for the first time in Dionysius: *divinization*. This harks back to Philo. The mind in the spirit of humanity is infused with the Logos, the mind in the spirit of God. This is what it is to be one with God and it renders us like God: divinized. (There are those who would argue that this line of reason leads directly to the monophysite heresy, condemned at the Council of Chalcedar, 451.)

Instrumental Images
    Hierarchy.

Terminal Images
    Mystery.
    Divinization.

SELECT BIBLIOGRAPHY
Dionysius the Areopagite, *Divine Names and Mystical Theology,* translated by C. E. Rolt. Allenson, 1972.

Reaction to Mysticism

The tradition of Alexandrian spirituality was deflected by historical events; to wit: the christological controversies of the fourth through seventh centuries in which some spiritual masters chose the losing side, and the rise of Islam in the seventh and eighth centuries. It also met a reaction within Christian spirituality itself.

First, the school in Antioch repudiated its highly speculative, highly apophatic commitment. As part of an anti-Origen movement they attacked his allegorical method of exegesis, replacing it with an equally bizarre typological method. Mysticism was replaced with a kataphatic, affective ascetical moralism. JOHN CHRYSOSTOM (c.347–407; Feast day: January 27), the very austere patriarch of Constantinople, embodies the worst and best of this school. Like most writers of the period, he was all in favor of virginity. He could be a bigoted misogynist. At the same time he could say some beautiful things about marriage. His spirituality is less monastic and more priestly. He was, however, a prototypical puritan, with none of the excitement of the mystics and a "works" mentality in the name of grace.

Second, there was a glimmer of protest against the repudiation of the created world by Alexandrian spirituality. This protest makes even contemporary writers, such as Bouyer, nervous. He admonishes his readers against paganism. The key figure was SYNESIUS OF CYRENE (c.370–c.414), bishop of Ptolemais, an honest, human lover of letters, the hunt, his wife, and the Lord (not necessarily in that order). Bouyer calls him an "intellectual sybarite." He had a profound spirituality, influenced by Neo-Platonic categories, but refused to repudiate the beauty of the natural world. He died a peaceful death, despite his willingness to be martyred by the barbarians. But his teacher, Hypatia, was murdered by the Christians of Alexandria. Synesius' work, *Dion,* is a defense of learning and reasonable pleasures. His *De Insomniis* is on the interpretation of dreams. He sounds like a man born before his time—or maybe a needed witness against the anti-intellectualism and Manicheanism that constantly threatens Christian spirituality.

So that Synesius may not be dismissed too lightly, the reader might recall some familiar lines from *The Hymnal 1940* of the Episcopal Church, which Allen Chatfield translated from a poem by this spiritual master of the early fifth century.

Lord Jesus, think on me,
   And purge away my sin;

From earth-born passions set me free,
    And make me pure within.

Lord Jesus, think on me,
    With care and woe opprest;
Let me thy loving servant be,
    And taste thy promised rest.

Lord Jesus, think on me,
    Nor let me go astray;
Through darkness and perplexity
    Point thou the heavenly way.

Lord Jesus, think on me,
    That, when the flood is past,
I may the eternal brightness see,
    And share thy joy at last.

The Hymnal 1940, 417

Are these the words of an "intellectual sybarite?"

SELECT BIBLIOGRAPHY

John Chrysostom, *Baptismal Instruction,* translated by Paul W. Harkins. (Ancient Christian Writers, Vol. 81) Paulist Press, 1963.

————, *Commentary on Saint John, the Apostle and Evangelist,* translated by Sr. Thomas Aquinas Goggin. (Fathers of the Church, Vols. 33,41) Catholic University Press, 1957, 1960.

————, *Homilies on the Sermon on the Mount,* edited by Jaroslav Pelikan. Fortress, 1967.

————, *The Priesthood,* translated by W. A. Jurgens. Macmillan, 1955.

Synesius, *Letters,* translated by Augustine FitzGerald. Oxford, 1926.

The Ancient West

Western Christian spirituality up to Augustine was an import from the East. The Western mind tends to be more kataphatic and affective—but there are notable exceptions throughout history—and so there is a tendency to popularize and soften.

AMBROSE (c. 339–397; Feast day: December 7) tempers the ascetical virtue of virginity with a lovely mystical image of the nuptial marriage. It is still virginity, however! He introduces a little casuistry with the assistance of Stoic ethics to ease the demands of the ascetical life. The controversial, unattractive Jerome was another typically Western man, who despised the mystics and advocated the historical study of the Scriptures.

The key figure, however, is AUGUSTINE (354–430: Feast day: August 28). We must always keep in mind that the Western church has, almost until the present, read the Fathers of the East through the filter of Augustine. This is for good and for bad. The one exception was in the ninth century, when Dionysius was translated by John Duns Scotus, known as Erigena, and became available to the West.

Augustine was the son of a demanding Christian mother, Monica. Jung would call her a "negative mother." He was trained as a teacher of rhetoric, was early a Manichean, and was converted to Christianity by means of his readings in the Neo-Platonists. Only later in his life, when he became bishop of Hippo, did he become more deeply steeped in the Scriptures and liturgy of the church. He never lost his heritage, although it became somewhat tempered. His own autobiography is a marvelous testimony to his struggle for the vision of God amid constant temptations of his senses. Clearly he believed that the way to God is by a repudiation of sensible reality through the inward journey within the self and then to the God who is *beyond* self.

The whole pattern of Augustine's life and the controversies he faced, particularly Pelagianism, would apparently lead him to reject the Eastern notion of deification or divinization. There is no *metachoria* (compenetration), as Gregory of Nyssa taught, for Augustine. Yet he speaks of God "deifying" humanity, just as he justifies humanity. Augustinian mysticism is of a personal God, encountered communally (again opposed to Gregory of Nyssa) within the mystical Body of Christ, the church. He was not much for visions save of the intellect. God gives light to the mind. The mind perceives God or light and the light leads to virtue. He finds Gregory's notion of darkness strange. The Christian quest is to appropriate in eternity what was first given us at our baptism. But as long as we are in the mortal body, we are constantly pulled back to earth. We have only a foretaste, which feeds our hope. What we become aware of is grace, which is the promise of eternal salvation.

Augustine's asceticism was part of the never-ending battle against concupiscence, the disordered inclination of fallen humanity toward the pleasure of the senses and, more particularly, sex. Man can do nothing without grace. In this Augustine seemed to go against the vocabulary of *synergy* of Gregory of Nyssa, but had difficulty overcoming the dangers of quietism—i.e., a purely passive spirituality. For Augustine the gift of grace is love of God and neighbor, called charity. Cupidity is the love of this world and age. There is nothing in Augustine which corresponds to *eros*. The love of God takes hold only as we become a question to ourselves, and then we must love only God as an end in himself and all else as a means to that end or, as in the case of a neighbor, a relative end.

In his treatise on the Trinity Augustine explains the nature of God in terms of charity. It naturally follows from this that God is charity, and for us to love rightly we simply participate in God. This has been called the "mystical moralism" of Augustine, and it manifests itself in our pastoral concern for others. Asceticism is dominated by pastoral care.

The mature spirituality of Augustine is found principally in the *Enarrationes,* the explanation of the psalms. They are a dialogue between the church as the bride and the Christ as the bridegroom. In his earlier *De Quantitate Animae* he provides a more analytical approach to the growth of the person. He says there are seven degrees of spiritual growth, which correspond to the consistent pattern in Christian spirituality to describe the ladder of ascent: mere animation, sense life, intellectual life or art, virtue and the moral life, tranquillity, entrance into divine light or the gaze of the purified soul upon God, and the vision of truth. For those who wish a more Neo-Platonic understanding of Augustine's teaching this is an example. It does not, however, reflect his thinking at the end of his life.

JOHN CASSIAN (c.360–435), a contemporary of Augustine, brought Eastern monasticism to the West. He is a fascinating person. His spirituality moves from apophatic/affective to kataphatic/affective, and occasionally flirts with apophatic/speculative. In some ways one gets the impression that his spiritual teaching is more balanced than Augustine's, less influenced by controversy. He lives at a time when *apatheia* and *gnōsis* are suspect because of the rise of anti-Origenism and suspicion of the Pelagians. But he makes the same point, uniting *apatheia* to the concept of charity (as in Augustine). He is able to use the rich imagery that comes from regular reflection upon the Scriptures, and at the same time he is an advocate of monologistic prayer. His favorite form is "O God, come to my assistance. Lord, make haste to help me."

Two images are of particular interest in Cassian. The first is the *fire of love*. It is his way of speaking of the presence of God and seems to be related to the prayer of the heart, as described particularly by the Eastern Fathers, especially the hesychasts. It is the result of an asceticism, which Cassian describes as the renunciation in three stages: deprivation, humility, and patience. This same image will play an important role in the writings of the fourteenth-century English mystic, Richard Rolle. It may be related to a sense of warmth, or even heat, often reported in mystical experiences.

The second image is *discretion*. Discretion means tempering ascetical practices in the light of a goal. Discretion is the "golden mean" of asceticism. "We ought then with all our might, to strive for the virtue of discretion by the power of humility, as it will keep us uninjured by either extreme, for there is an old saying, . . . extremes meet. For excess of fasting and gluttony come to the same thing" (*Conferences*, 2:16). When Eastern methods were brought to the West the tendency was to go overboard. Cassian reminds us that asceticism is a means to an end and has value only as it opens us to the presence of God.

Seemingly in contradiction to discretion, Cassian suffers from an excessive notion of the nature of sin—e.g., an involuntary distraction in prayer is for him a sin—and would avoid works of charity on behalf of a neighbor if it stands in the way of ascetical practice.

BENEDICT OF NURSIA (c.480–c.550; Feast day: July 11), the founder of the Benedictine Order, goes further than Cassian in the westernization of Christian spirituality. We know Benedict from his rule, which is the epitome of discretion. It is written against the wandering monk. Therefore, the images it advances are *stability, obedience,* and *humility.* The monk stays attached to his monastery and lives in community. He is absolutely obedient to the abbot, who is elected for life and who is his spiritual "father." Humility, which is the openness to grace, is the mother of perfection. In this he is indebted to Cassian.

For Benedict, the work of God, the *Opus Dei,* is the *daily recitation of the Divine Office.* His spirituality, which is kataphatic and affective—as is all Benedictine spirituality since then—is fed by the reading of the Scriptures, particularly the psalms, in community. The influence of Benedictine spirituality upon the English church dates from the coming of Augustine of Canterbury, a Benedictine monk, to bring Christianity to the Anglo-Saxons in 597. The place of the daily Office will always occupy a prominent place in English spirituality up until this very day.

Instrumental Images
   Grace to fight concupiscence.
   Self-questioning.
   Discretion.

THE EARLY CHURCH 47

Stability, obedience, humility.
Recitation of the Divine office, the *Opus Dei*.

Terminal Images
Charity.
Fire of Love.

SELECT BIBLIOGRAPHY
Ambrose, *Complete Letters,* translated by Mary Melchior Beyenka. (Fathers of the Church, Vols. 26, 28) Catholic University Press, 1954.
————, *Creation, Paradise, Cain and Abel,* translated by John J. Savage. (Fathers of the Church, Vol. 42). Catholic University Press, 1961.

The writings of Augustine of Hippo abound. The beginner can profit from reading the *Confessions* and *On the Trinity*. Unfortunately, the *Explanations of the Psalms* is not readily available in an English translation. Two introductory selections of Augustine's writings are:

An Augustine Reader, edited by John J. O'Meara. Image Books, 1973.
The Essential Augustine, edited by Vernon J. Bourke. New American Library, 1973.
Benedict, *Rule,* translated by J. McCann. Christian Classics, 1972.
John Cassian, *Conferences.* (Nicene and Post-Nicene Church Fathers, series ii, Vol. 11). Eerdmans, n.d.
————, *Teachings.* Eastern Orthodox, n.d.

·II·

The Middle Ages (500–1000)

The Heroic Age (500–1000)

GREGORY THE GREAT (540–604; Feast day: March 11), a Benedictine, is the father of Western spirituality in the Middle Ages;
so while he really belongs to the ancient world, we mention him
here. He is kataphatic and borderline speculative/affective.

The terminal image Gregory uses most is the vision of God,
which is a vision of light. He divides this vision into two kinds:
desire and rapture. He is not always clear what the difference is,
although rapture is fleeting and desire is unfading. Both indicate
we are called to *see* God. The word "contemplation" in various
uses, but always as an act of seeing, permeates his writings.
When later in medieval piety we read definitions of contemplation as a form of seeing, we need to keep this approach of
Gregory's in mind. It appears that where Eastern mysticism,
which is a more feminine spirituality, focuses on the receptive
heart, Western mysticism, which is more masculine, focuses on
the action of the eyes. We strive for the vision of God—what the
late bishop of Oxford, Kenneth Kirk (1886–1954), called the
summam bonam, "the highest good," in his classic work by the
title, *The Vision of God*. Western spirituality is very much in the
debt of Gregory the Great in this way.

An instrumental image in Gregory is *servitude,* which epitomizes his ascetical doctrine. Humanity—an image important to

Gregory—achieves purification as it characterizes the Christian who does his duty of service, including pastoral care. Service embodies virtue, and virtue is a condition of the interior life. The interior life is described as purity of heart, but in a Western sense, not in the Eastern notion of affection of heart. The heart, the center of the self, sees the judgments of God and develops humility, patience, repentance. Humility is the generic virtue, which makes possible compunction or awareness of guilt. We do penance, confessing our sins, patiently following Christ. All this gives us detachment, which opens us to the vision of God.

There is something very "Western" about Gregory: the emphasis upon the vision of God, service (including pastoral care) as integral to the spiritual life, humility and guilt, and the quest of detachment. It is "Western," not so much because Gregory was Western but because the West followed Gregory when it was not under the spell of Dionysius.

It might be noted here that the principal interpreter of Gregory to the medieval church was ISIDORE (c.560–636), the archbishop of Seville. His *Sententiarum Libri Tres,* "Three Books of Sentences," which is the main source for his work on Gregory, awaits an English translation. He, together with the VENERABLE BEDE (c.625–735; Feast day: May 25), developed an ascetical practice which involved reading, meditation, prayer, and intention—*lectio, meditatio, oratio,* and *intentio. Meditatio* is not what we may think it is, but involves memory of what was read and discussion of questions about it with the abbot. It was a very simple method, suitable for the barbarians. It is not unlike those highly kataphatic forms of meditation common to the seventeenth-century French church, which we draw upon today.

Just in passing, I need to mention a Greek theologian who became particularly important to the West, a contemporary of Isidore and Bede, MAXIMUS THE CONFESSOR (c.580–662). He was the first to give the classical form to the three ways to God—purgation, illumination, and union—which became the classic "ladder" for Western medieval spirituality. Bonaventure

(1221–1274) particularly will build on them. Actually the three steps under different names go back to Origen, and before him to Philo, who probably got it from the Greeks. The three ways are related to the prayer of the lips, mind, and heart of the Eastern monks. Maximus was strongly influenced by Evagrius Ponticus even though he describes him as that "abominable heretic." He was, in effect, an instrument for Evagrius' unknown influence in later centuries.

After Gregory, there are the barbarians. One must keep in mind the impact of this people, whose paganism was covered by a very thin veneer of Christian learning from the South and whose piety came out of animism and the world of magic—if it *ever* truly went beyond its origins. Such spirituality tended more toward objects—e.g., the Cross, the Real Presence in the Eucharist, the Blessed Virgin, the Scriptures—than the subtleties of process—e.g., growth in perfection. *The whole shape of Western spirituality is a function of this radically new Germanic culture with a strong addition of Celtic culture.*

One of the enigmas of church history yet to be sufficiently explored is the impact of Celtic Christianity on the West. Christianity was planted in Roman Britain and beyond in the second or third centuries by nameless missionaries, and grew among the poor. It was strongly monastic in character, with an accompanying ascetical bent. The Celts had a very real sense of the spiritual powers and were concerned to protect themselves against the forces of evil by invoking the forces of good. The penitential system of the Celtic church shaped the sacrament of penance during this period, with the growth of specific penances exacted for specific sins and the weighing of the gravity of a given sin on the basis of criteria such as the social status of the sinner and the one sinned against. The prayer known as the "breastplate"—Hymn 268 in *The Hymnal 1940*, probably incorrectly attributed to Patrick, is the best known example—was characteristic of Celtic piety. It served to ward off the evil spirits, hence the word "breastplate." The Celts had a deep devotion to the Gospels, carrying copies of them around with them. The lovely Book of

Kells, now housed in Trinity College, Dublin, is an outstanding eighth-century example.

It is the time of the "Christian hero," who by his asceticism witnessed to his faith—an asceticism sometimes lacking in discretion. It was in the monasteries, as we know, that spirituality burned most brightly in the Heroic Age, but not without the influence of the outside world. The Divine Office fed the monks, and the Psalter shaped the mind and heart of the participants.

A reading of the hymnody of this period gives us a clue to the imagery of the times. An example would be Hymn 123 from The Hymnal 1940 by RABANUS MAURUS (776 or 784–856), one of the greatest theologians of the Carolingian period.

> Christ, the fair glory of the holy angels,
>   Maker of all men, ruler of all nations,
> Grant of thy mercy unto us thy servants
>   Steps up to heaven.

The hymn then invokes the archangels Michael, Gabriel, and Raphael, and concludes as follows:

> May the blest Mother of our Lord and Saviour,
>   May the celestial company of angels,
> May the assembly of the saints in heaven,
>   Help us to praise thee.

> Father Almighty, Son, and Holy Spirit,
>   God ever blessed, hear our thankful praises;
> Thine is the glory which from all creation
>   Ever ascendeth.

The reference to the ladder—i.e., steps—is predictable. Also the spheres of heaven, governed by the archangels in particular, reminds us of Dionysius. Rabanus wrote a treatise on prayer in which the first book was "On seeing God" and the second book was "On purity of heart"—very common themes in Western spirituality.

Prominent figures are rare at this time in the West. The Carolingian renewal in the ninth century was a time of new interest in the Scriptures and the liturgy. By this time medieval society had formed into three divisions: laity, religious, and clerics. The Benedictine monk was the prototypical religious, and the emphasis for him was on the Divine Office. Solitary prayer was not the rule, and the advice was that one should only pray briefly alone, unless one was given to tears—a sign of a deeper spiritual vocation. Otherwise one might be overcome by evil thoughts.

This being true, it is not surprising that there was an emphasis upon the memorization and use of verbal, kataphatic—as distinguished from monologistic—prayer. The Our Father, the Hail Mary, the *Gloria patri,* and particularly the memorization of the psalms takes on a new importance.

The piety for the lay person was patterned after that of the monks. The clerics were now organized—Chrodegang of Metz (d. 766), a pre-Carolingian reformer and a name to be remembered, wrote an *ordo canonicus* which sought to pattern the lives of the diocesan priests as much as possible after the rule of Benedict. The priests were pushed more and more into the monastic mold. This process would continue for centuries. The spirituality of the monk was clearly the ideal. It was designed for tribal (i.e., community) life, not the anchoritic life of the Egyptian desert.

In 850 an Irishman called JOHN SCOTUS or ERIGENA (c.810–877), showed up in the court of the Frankish king, Charles the Bald. Erigena became the interpreter of Greek mystical thought for the West. He translated Dionysius, Maximus the Confessor, and Gregory of Nyssa, and wrote treatises on them. He was a Neo-Platonist and introduced that philosophy to the West. It is not surprising that Erigena was apophatic and speculative. He taught that there are degrees of knowing—sense, discernment of hidden realities, and illumination by God—which lead to our return (*reversio*) to the God from which we came forth. This emphasis upon the return will reappear in the mysticism of the fourteenth century. Erigena speaks of deification. Christ sums up the perfect humanity.

Erigena was not only unappreciated in his time, he was suspected of heresy. He was an influence later in the twelfth century, particularly on William of St. Thierry. In the thirteenth century, however, he was accused of pantheism, a common risk in the West of apophatic/speculative mystical theologians. An age like the Heroic, which is heavy on asceticism, penitence, and mortification, is not likely to find someone of Erigena's bent very compatible.

Instrumental Images
   Servitude.
   Humility, patience, repentance.
   Reading, meditation, prayer and intention.
   Purgation, insight, union.
   The life of the monk.
   Detachment.

Terminal Images
   Vision of God.

SELECT BIBLIOGRAPHY

Bede, *Ecclesiastical History of the English Nation,* translated by John Stevens. Dutton, 1973.

Gregory, *Ascetical Works,* translated by Virginia Woods Callahan. (Fathers of the Church, Vol. 58) Catholic University Press, n.d.

————, *Pastoral Care,* translated by Henry Davis. Newman, 1950.

John Scotus Erigena, *Periphyseon,* translated by I. P. Sheldon-Williams L. Bieler. 1968.

Maximus the Confessor, *The Ascetical Life and the Four Centuries on Charity,* translated by Polycarp Sherwood. (Ancient Christian Writers, Vol. 21) Catholic University Press, 1965.

The High Middle Ages (1000–1300)

In the first half of the tenth century monastic reform was insti-
tuted at Cluny and deeply influenced all of monasticism in
France. In the eleventh century it continued, with a real challenge to the Benedictine ideal of the community life. There was a
longing for silence and solitude. Despite the monastery, the wandering hermit had become a frequent feature of the West. There
was a need to abate the plethora of peripatetic recluses, while
honoring the quest for simple solitude. This need was met,
among other ways, with the creation of the monastery at Char-
treuse by Bruno in 1084, the beginning of the Carthusians—a
balanced, sincere, but rigorous group indeed. The creation of a
number of new monastic foundations like the Carthusians—who
differed from the Benedictine inasmuch as they were more clois-
tered, contemplative, and austere—was an effort to give order to
this longing for solitude. Private prayer was introduced into
monastic rule and a greater interiorization of the spirit evolved.

One of the great Carthusians, GUIGO II (died c.1193), described the four degrees of exercises of the spirit. The order is
very interesting and should be noted carefully. "Seek in *reading*
and you will find in *meditation;* knock by *prayer* and it will be
opened to you in *contemplation."* First comes reading, then meditation, then prayer, and finally contemplation. All this was
kataphatic and affective.

With the call for the First Crusade in 1095 by Urban II the
long-standing fondness of Western people for pilgrimages became
institutionalized on a much grander scale. At the same time
Urban II's predecessor, Gregory VII (c.1021–1085) had insti-
tuted his famous reform, which pushed ever harder for the secular
clergy to follow the spirituality of the religious.

"The most remarkable medieval spiritual author before St. Ber-
nard" and the pivotal figure between the Heroic Age and the
High Middle Ages was the eleventh-century Benedictine, JOHN
OF FECAMP. His writings were among the most influential in the

medieval world until, in the fifteenth century, he was displaced by Thomas à Kempis. Yet no one knows him. He was torn between action and contemplation, the life of the hermit and the reform of communities. He emphasized heavily the importance of reading and used to send written prayers to his friends. In Fecamp's theology God was far off but Jesus mediated his presence, particularly in the Eucharist. His piety was intensely affective, and it strongly influenced the medieval emphasis upon the humanity of our Lord.

ANSELM (c. 1033–1109; Feast day: April 21), a great theologian and a spiritual master in the Benedictine tradition, paved the way for Bernard. His struggle was between love and intellect, so he is not as affective as John of Fecamp. He is also a good bit more austere. He truly believed that reason had a compelling force which leads us to God. He was the "door" to the twelfth and thirteenth centuries, particularly Scholasticism.

In 1098 the Cistercian Order was founded at Citeaux. The man who did the most to establish that order was BERNARD OF CLAIRVAUX (1090–1153; Feast day: August 20). He was a man deeply steeped in the Scriptures. He particularly liked to dwell on the story of Jesus. His *Sermons on the Canticle* are well known. His exegetical method was Origen's and Augustine's. While not an original intellect, he had a grasp of theology. He knew Gregory of Nyssa and probably read some Dionysius, but the latter is of no influence. He was above all a monk who practiced self-mortification but was not given to visions. He was a concrete, medieval man of contemplation and action.

For Bernard free will—which is really free consent—and God's grace meet to bestow a love that produces good fruit in humanity. This begins with humility that begets a sense of our poverty and our dignity as a baptized person, which leads to three steps toward freedom to love God: (1) the absence of compulsion to sin, *libertas a necessitate;* (2) the possibility of choosing, even to sin, *libertas a peccato;* (3) the inability to sin, *posse non peccare.* We do not reach the third stage until heaven. The entire advance is made possible by the love of God, which dominates Bernard's thought. He is kataphatic and affective.

This is very clearly shown in this excerpt from his *Sermons on the Canticle*.

> 'My Beloved is mine, and I am His, Who feeds among the lilies.' . . . The Bride is not unmindful that He Who feeds is also He Who makes His flock to feed; and that He Who abides among the lilies is the Same as He Who reigns above the stars. But she prefers to call His humbleness to mind, not only because she loves humility, but also because it was when He began to feed as one of the flock that He first became her Beloved; it was indeed the fact of His doing so that made Him dear to her. For He is her Lord in His loftiness and her Beloved in His lowliness; he reigns above the stars and loves among the lilies. Even above the stars He loved; for He is love, and never and nowhere can He do otherwise than love (30,iii)

This brief passage illustrates Bernard's style of biblical exegesis: the centrality of Jesus as mediator, the focus on love as all encompassing, and a highly affective approach. We need to keep in mind how this passage dominates the medieval piety that is influenced by Bernard.

Love so dominates Bernard's thinking that it is the central theme of his mystical theology. "The God who is desired and loved becomes [for Bernard] the God of desire and love." Christ is our bridegroom. His kiss is the Holy Spirit. Medieval piety is universally conditioned by this belief of Bernard's. It and the mysticism of the Trinity, which begins with Bernard but is developed by William of St. Thierry, will characterize Western spirituality for the next four hundred years.

Bernard believed you could not be saved without being a Christian—and it was hard without also being a Cistercian. His asceticism is summed up in what has influenced Cistercians such as Thomas Merton ever since: remembrance and imitation. A key word for him, which is as old as Tertullian in Christian spirituality, is *devotio,* "devotion." It describes total commitment. Particularly, one practiced devotion to the humanity of Christ, as John of Fecamp suggested before Bernard. It is in the spirit of devotion that we read the Divine Office, participate in the Eucharist, and read the Scriptures. If we do this we may be *visited by the Word,* that momentary glimpse of the highest form of contemplation. Whereas Anselm (c.1033–1109) spoke of *fides quaerens intellectum,* "faith seeking understanding," St. Bernard spoke of *animaquaerens Verbum,* "soul seeking Word." The first is speculative, the second affective.

WILLIAM OF ST. THIERRY (c.1085–1148) is an important figure who has existed too long in the shadow of Bernard. He was a Benedictine who lived in a Cistercian house and wrote for the Carthusians. He greatly admired Bernard, but the latter would not permit him at Clairvaux. He was strongly influenced by Origen, Gregory of Nyssa, and, as already noted, Erigena. He wanted to revitalize Augustinian thought, which had become ossified. Consequently, he is more speculative than Bernard, but has that Western medieval emphasis on love.

Like most medieval theologians, he believed that the image of God was not totally destroyed in man and there was a natural tendency in man for God, which is a natural love. The ascent to God is to become *like* God. (Un-natural love is a result of the Fall.) Asceticism shapes and directs natural love so that humanity is touched by the love of God and made perfect. "Love itself is knowledge; love itself is understanding," writes William. But this is an intellectual love, not a psychological—one might almost say "sentimental"—love as in Bernard.

William adopted the psychology of Origen. Humanity consisted of soul, mind, and spirit. The union with God was analogous to the physiology of sight, as William and others understood it in their day. Sight consisted of the spirit traveling from the brain, down the optic nerve, out through the eyeball and meeting the spirit of the object seen. There the spirits comingled and colors and shapes were transferred to the spirit from the eye, which was carried back to the brain for reflection. In like manner the human spirit, the highest part of humanity, engaged the spirit of God. This was called "compenetration," as in Gregory of Nyssa. It also revealed the medieval person's belief that there was a consistency between the process of nature and the supernatural.

Elsewhere William writes,

> But when serious thought is properly devoted to serious matters, the will, acting on the free deliberations of reason, calls forth from the memory whatever is needed, applies the intellect to the memory to form a concept, and when it is formed, such as it may be, the intellect submits it to the examination of the subject: so it is that the process of thought is completed.

This may sound like a discussion of theological method, which it is; but it is much more. It is a statement of William's belief that the exercise of memory, reason, and will leads us to contemplate God. Progress in the spiritual life comes through the santification of memory, reason or understanding, and will. These categories go back to Augustine. They will appear again and again in medieval and early modern mystics. Ignatius Loyola will develop these faculties of the mind methodologically in the sixteenth century. Through such santification humanity must move from the animal to the rational and on to the spiritual existence. The prayer of the lips, the mind, and the heart (the triple sign of the cross on the forehead, mouth, and chest, at the announcing of the Gospel in the Eucharist is an enactment of this prayer) has a certain resonance here, but Western man is more likely to be affective and kataphatic—even after reading Origen, Gregory, and Erigena.

William's contribution extends further in the *mysticism of the Holy Trinity.* He compared memory to the Father, reason to the Son, and love to the Holy Spirit. When memory, reason, and love are possessed by God, they possess the likeness of God—a play on "the image and likeness of God" found in Irenaeus almost a thousand years before. Somehow the power that sustains this movement from sin to unity with the Trinity is faith. In fact faith is a form of reason—*a ratio fidei* ("by reason of faith"), whose method is love. It is only replaced by vision. This is an important concept, which is present in contemporary Roman Catholic spirituality (e.g., Bernard Lonergan).

One of William of St. Thierry's much earlier readers and admirers, however, was Julian of Norwich, a fourteenth-century anchorite who shared his optimism and his mysticism of the Trinity.

AELRED OF RIEVAULX (1109–1167), who first made the outward journey of the itinerant hermit an analogy of the inner journey of the Christian ascetic or person of prayer, was called the "Bernard of the North." He was an Englishman and is either an early precursor of the character of English piety or he made a lasting impact upon it. He seems to have been the Christian counterpart of the Roman Cicero, who was certainly read by all educated men of his time. For Aelred has a real spiritual concern for friendship. It is a way to Christ.

> In friendship are joined honor and charm, truth and joy, sweetness, and good-will, affection and action. And all these take their beginning from Christ, advance through Christ, and are perfected in Christ. Therefore, not too unnatural or too steep does the ascent appear from Christ, as the inspiration of the love by which we love our friend, as Christ giving himself to us as our Friend for us to love, so that charm may follow upon charm, sweetness upon sweetness, and affection upon affection. And thus, friend cleaving to friend in the spirit of Christ, is made with Christ but one heart and one soul, and so mounting aloft through degrees of love to friendship with Christ.

This is a more affective piety than one finds in William of St. Thierry.

Instrumental Images
   Reading, meditation, prayer, and contemplation.
   Inner journey.
   Pilgrimage.
   Written prayers.
   Reason.
   Devotion (remembrance and imitation).
   Faith, *a ratio fidei.*
   Silence and solitude.
   Friendship.

Terminal Images
   Posse non peccare.
   Mysticism of the Holy Trinity.
   Visitation by the Word.

SELECT BIBLIOGRAPHY
Aelred of Rievaulx, *The Mirror of Charity,* translated by Geoffrey
   Webb and Adrian Walker. Mowbray, 1962.
————, *Spiritual Friendship,* translated by Mary Eugenia Laker.
   Cistercian Publications, 1974.
Anselm, *Basic Writings,* translated by Sidney N. Dean. Open
   Court, 1974.
Bernard, *On the Song of Songs,* translated by Kilian Walsh. 2 Vols.
   Cistercian Publications, 1976.
————, *Treatise on Loving God: On the Steps of Humility.* Cistercian
   Publications, 1974.
William of St. Thierry, *Works.* 5 Vols. to date. Cistercian Publi-
   cations, 1974–1978.

The Schoolmen

One needs to be familiar with the school of St. Victor in Paris
and its two most distinguished representatives: Hugh and Richard. The influence of Victorine piety on later medieval mystics is

impressive. It was kataphatic, but while Hugh was predominantly affective, Richard was more speculative.

HUGH OF ST. VICTOR (c. 1096–1141), a great synthesizer, believed that all learning was relevant to the experience of God and
that reason, while not sufficient, was consistent with affective
faith. Affective faith was the ultimate means to God. He read
Dionysius and wrote a commentary on the celestial hierarchy.

A thirteenth-century Victorine, Thomas Gallus, translated the
Mystical Theology of Dionysius. By a subtle *mis*-translation he
changes the darkness of intelligence in Dionysius into the darkness of love, shifting him from speculative to affective! This influenced all in the West that followed. It is particularly notice-
able in *The Cloud of Unknowing,* whose author some believe was
particularly dependent upon Gallus. The following quotation
from Hugh is an example of just such an emphasis.

> The foundation and basis of holy teaching is history, from
> which the truth of allegory is extracted like honey from the
> comb. If then, you are building, lay the foundation of history
> first; then by the typical sense put up a mental structure as a
> citadel of faith and finally, like a coat of loveliest of colours,
> paint the building with the elegance of morality. In the his-
> tory you have the deeds of God to wonder at, in allegory his
> mysteries to believe, in morality his perfection to imitate.

The logic of this procedure is that one begins with Scripture,
moves to theology, and concludes with ethics. The goal of all of
it is the contemplation of God.

What the life of Moses was to Origen and Gregory of Nyssa,
and the *Canticle* to almost everyone, Noah's Ark is to Hugh. He
wrote three treatises on the typology of the Ark. The Ark is the
human heart, which God commands to be built and in which
God dwells as knowledge and love. The speculative and affective
elements exist in relationship to one another in this highly kataphatic image. In this regard Hugh writes, "God is become everything to you, and God has made everything for you. He has

made the dwelling [the Ark], and it has become your refuge." He concludes by saying that it is "on account of this that the whole of scripture was made. For this the world was created. For this the Word was made flesh, God was made humble, man was made sublime."

Hugh, along with the other Victorines, made more of *lectio*, "divine reading," than anyone else. This focused on discovering the hiddenness of God in his world, and rested ultimately upon the reading of Scripture. In a general sense, however, it meant the *symbolic interpretation of the created order*. This was common to medieval piety, as will be mentioned again, but the Victorines made it a matter of principle.

Hugh's theology was christocentric, ecclesial, and sacramental. He taught a typical ascent to the knowledge of God, the fifth mode of which he describes as being "ravished by the extreme sweetness of tasting God, and no longer look at anything but God." The image of sweetness will occur again and again in succeeding centuries.

RICHARD OF ST. VICTOR (d. 1173) was a mystical theologian, who believed one could arrive at the essentials of Christian doctrine by speculative reason. While it is evident that he was deeply read in Dionysius, he modifies him for his own purposes. There are six levels of contemplation in Richard's system. The first two pertain to the imagination and have the "sensibles" as their object, the second two pertain to reason and have the "intelligibles" as their object, and the last two pertain to understanding and have the "intellectibles" as their object. The intellectibles are given to us by divine self-disclosure.

Richard's system begins with love, as is typical of Victorine thought, since its members followed Augustine and Bernard. Richard's four degrees of love were quoted widely for centuries afterward: love that wounds the soul, binds the soul, makes the soul languish, and causes it to swoon. At the height of contemplation the soul penetrates the realm of wisdom; so it is the rational soul, as in Neo-Platonism, to which God gives understanding. A key Bible verse for Richard is Psalm 68:27, "There is Benjamin, a youth in ecstasy of mind." (This is a translation of the latin translation of the Hebrew. It does not appear like this in our Bibles.) There is a speculative element, therefore, that anticipates the fourteenth-century Rhineland mystics.

Among the fascinating constructs which appear in Richard is his discussion of *discretion,* a notion that anticipates discernment. "We must be practiced," Richard writes,

> in individual virtues and what we are able to undertake in each one of them before we are able to comprehend full knowledge concerning all of them and to judge sufficiently concerning individual ones.

To be able to do this is to practice discretion, which comes, in one sense, from reading, listening, reasoning, and above all experiencing. In another sense, says Richard, "discretion is born from reason alone."

Richard is widely quoted, by both Franciscans and Dominicans in the thirteenth century, and is a profound influence on the fourteenth-century mystics, including Julian of Norwich.

Although it may appear rather farfetched to some, there is a possible relationship between the Victorines and the Protestant Reformation at its best. Among the Victorines' admirers was John Tauler, the fourteenth-century mystic. Tauler, in turn, was read by Martin Luther and his followers. Victorine theology was biblical, not philosophical, in its roots. For example, Richard writes, "Every truth that the auhority of Scripture does not confirm is suspect to me." As Hugh of St. Victor argued, the knowledge of God is a knowledge of faith—first of piety, then approved by reason, and finally experienced by taste. Without love there can be no faith. Much of this resonates with what was taught four hundred years later.

It needs to be noted, however, that the Victorines were medieval men. Unlike the reformers, they believed in a continuity between nature and supernature and a progression in faith that results from ascetical discipline. Richard's discussion of ecstasy would be much too rich for the blood of a reformer.

Instrumental Images
   Symbolic interpretation of the created order

SELECT BIBLIOGRAPHY
Hugh of St. Victor, *Selected Spiritual Writings*. Harper & Row, 1962.

Popular Piety

The twelfth century was the time of Henry II, Thomas à Becket, Richard the Lionhearted, and Robin Hood. Monastic spirituality made its impact on the people at a time when there was religious unrest; a strange quest for purity and a moral laxity at the same time with the same people, and a consecration of the profession of arms (the religious ceremonies surrounding the "dubbing" of the knight).

Devotion centered, as we have already indicated, on the humanity of Christ: particularly in terms of the Holy Name of Jesus, the Blessed Sacrament, and the Sacred Heart of Jesus. We owe the emphasis upon the last named to the Cistercians and particularly, despite his speculative bent, to Richard of St. Victor. Actually the Sacred Heart does not take on a certain saccharine quality until after the fourteenth century.

Marian devotion prospered at the popular level. The theory of the Immaculate Conception and the Assumption were widely believed, although theologians carefully avoided discussing them. Actually a whole feminine element appears in the piety, which is also expressed in the emergence of romantic love—i.e., *eros*—as in the practice of the "courts of love" and in the popular literature.

Demons, angels, and saints became very important. Veneration of the saints, which in the thirteenth century inspires pilgrimages to holy places (as in the Crusades), was widely observed. Medieval people believed that everything—particularly the unusual—was an evidence of the numinous. The word "monster" comes from the Latin *monstrare,* meaning to "demonstrate" the numinous. (The word "monstrance," an item designed for the exposition of the Blessed Sacrament, also comes from *monstrare,* but that dates from the fourteenth century and the institution of Benediction of the Blessed Sacrament.)

Keep in mind that the piety of the twelfth century is highly biblical, but it looks for the hidden meaning, as in Origen and all who followed him.

Instrumental Images

Devotion to the humanity of Jesus (Holy Name, Blessed Sacrament, Sacred Heart).

Reflection of the feminine.

Veneration of the saints.

The Friars

The rise of the Franciscan and Dominican friars—the word means "brothers," and they are to be distinguished from "monks" who live in monasteries (e.g., the Benedictines, the Carthusians, the Cistercians, etc.)—in the thirteenth century changes the religious scene dramatically. The friars, Franciscan or Dominican, were kataphatic. The former were more affective and the latter more speculative, as a rule.

Everyone knows the figure of FRANCIS OF ASSISI (1181–1226; Feast day: October 4), who married "Lady Poverty" and loved Christ, the Gospel, and the church with an unremitting passion. He was devoted to preaching, penance, and prayer. He had a deep sense of communion with the natural order, particularly death (the older depiction of Francis is not preaching to the birds but holding a skull). He was remarkably successful in establishing an order. With Francis medieval piety is summarized. It was concrete, particular, human, and moral. There was a profound devotion to the humanity of Jesus which, if it got out of hand, could (and later did) develop into sentimental pietism. With Francis there was a profound devotion to the crucified Christ, which anticipated the grim realistic art of the fourteenth and fifteenth centuries. Francis, however, was more typical of the ethereal luminosity of twelfth- and thirteenth-century religious art, as in Giotto. Francis began the devotion to the infant Jesus, to which we can trace the contemporary crib or *crèche*.

The greatest of the Franciscan teachers of the spiritual life was BONAVENTURE (1217–1274). Bonaventure was a systemizer in spirituality as Thomas Aquinas was in theology and Dante in medieval culture. He was influenced by Augustine and Dionysius. He is known as the "second founder" of the Franciscans, promoting a spirit of intellectual inquiry in the order. He teaches a balanced spirituality with even some apophatic elements. His purpose is the "re-creation" of the soul as a product of grace. The necessity of poverty as an openness to grace is obvious in the Franciscan.

Bonaventure's best known contribution is the description of the ascent of the soul in *De triplici via* (*Concerning the Triple Way*). He gives the definitive definition for the West of the three ways of meditation: purgation, illumination, and union. Purgation requires that a person "exercise himself on the use of the sting of conscience." Its goal is a clean conscience. In illumination "the beam of intelligence shed light upon our darkness." We are reminded of the promises of God. In union we raise aloft "the little flame of wisdom" and come to face the God who is "inconceivable; yet He is all delight." Bonaventure does not define union or contemplation. He is dependent upon Hugh of St. Victor, who says it is "a free, penetrating, and fixed gaze." Then he makes the striking comment from a more apophatic mode. "Our mind . . . when it glimpses the light of the supreme Being, seems to itself to see nothing."

As in all medieval spiritual masters, prayer follows meditation. In *The Tree of Life* Bonaventure describes an act of meditation which anticipates Ignatius Loyola by three hundred years. "In prayer," he says elsewhere, "our interior affections are purified and we are united with the one 'true and highest good' as well as strengthened in virtue." It is important to note the three movements in prayer for Bonaventure. By prayer a person "should first deplore his misery (i.e., his sin), . . . second, implore God's mercy, . . . third, . . . render worship by displaying reverence, love and delight in God." There is no mention of intercession or petition.

The great Franciscan mystic was RAYMOND LULL (1235–1316), a converted troubadour. He is typical of Franciscan spirituality except that he speaks of contemplation as carried on by the orderly and methodical application of memory, understanding, and will. The spirituality of William of St. Thierry is recognizable here, and one wonders whether Ignatius Loyola read Lull or William. There is also a typical Franciscan fascination with the events in the life of Christ—conception, birth, childhood, passion, death—which has influenced Western piety from then to now.

Before his conversion in 1270 Lull was quite a ladies' man. In his principal work, *Book of Contemplation,* there is a curious Neo-Platonic dualism combined with a vocabulary clearly developed in the boudoir. Lull was fascinated by Muslim mysticism. His *Book of the Lover and the Beloved* is patterned after the manner of the sufis. One particular aphorism leaps out and meets the eye from this work:

> Said the Beloved to the Lover: "Knowest thou yet what love meaneth?" The Lover answered: "If I knew not the meaning of love, I should know the meaning of trial, sorrow and pain."

To understand the force of what Lull is saying one needs to remember that in the tradition of the medieval "courts of love" which spawned him, romantic love and death went hand-in-hand. Think of the aria "Liebestod" (*Love-death*) from Wagner's

Tristam und Isolde. Perhaps this gives us a better feel for what Lull and others meant when they said love made suffering bearable even though it demanded suffering, instead of our contemporary notion that love always leads to satisfaction and possession.

Lull died a martyr, trying to convert the Muslims.

DOMINIC (1173–1221; Feast day: August 8) founded the Dominicans, the Order of Preachers, to combat the rise of heresy. Like the Franciscans, his order held poverty as the supreme value, and consequently were also mendicants ("beggars"). The Dominicans are more speculative than the Franciscans. Preaching was the ostensible task, but they came to be the first to train seriously for *spiritual direction.* Of course, it had roots in earlier thought and practice. Abelard's (1079–1142) theology had made much of friendship just as did Aelred. Previously the practice of spiritual direction had been in the monastic model, and was generally believed to be needed only by beginners. "Discretion" followed direction. But now, with the Dominicans, spiritual direction was prescribed for everyone. Lay persons were often spiritual guides.

The great Dominican whom we all know is THOMAS AQUINAS (1224–1274; Feast day: January 28). He was a pupil of another Dominican, Albert the Great (1206–1280). Albert knew the limits of our knowledge of God and therefore had reservations about what mystical contemplation could accomplish. We cannot see God himself, he said, but only by means of abstract *species.* Remember that this is the thirteenth century and Aristotle is beginning to replace Plato as the premier pagan philosopher.

For Aquinas the intellect is "capable of God." The quest is of the spirit of light—not the darkness of Dionysius. Aquinas gives us a clear distinction between meditation and contemplation, although this distinction will not be followed by the founder of scientific spiritual theology, Ignatius Loyola. For Aquinas, meditation is reason, a discursive deduction from the principles of truth. Contemplation is a simple, intuitive, vision of truth. Contemplation is motivated by love. With Richard of St. Victor he holds that what one strives for in contemplation is the "clear gaze of the mind," which is very different from the Franciscans who emphasized wonder and will over intellect. Of course, Aquinas taught, as did his teacher Aristotle, that we never see the essence of God.

Instrumental Images
Poverty.
Preaching or listening to preaching.
Purgation, illumination, and union.
Consecration of memory, understanding, and will.
Spiritual direction.
Intellect.

Terminal Images
Free, penetrating, and fixed gaze.
Clear gaze of the mind.

SELECT BIBLIOGRAPHY

Bonaventure, *The Soul's Journey into God, The Tree of Life,* and *The Life of St. Francis,* translated by Ewert Cousins, Paulist Press, 1978.

Raymond Lull, *The Art of Contemplation,* translated by Allison Peers. Gordon Press, 1976.

————, *The Book of Beasts,* translated by Allison Peers. Hyperion, 1978.

————, *Book of the Lover and the Beloved,* translated by Allison Peers. Paulist, 1978.

————, *The Tree of Love,* translated by Allison Peers. Macmillan, 1926.

The works of Thomas Aquinas abound. The beginner might start with:

Introduction to Saint Thomas Aquinas, edited by Anton C. Pegis. Modern Library, 1948.

The Late Middle Ages (1300–1500)

It is impossible to understand the fourteenth and fifteenth centuries, and the Protestant and Roman Catholic Reformations that followed, unless we note the dramatic shift in outlook that occurs from the late thirteenth century into the fourteenth century, and play down the tendency to make the break between the fifteenth and sixteenth centuries too sharp. Much of what we attribute to the sixteenth century has its roots in the fourteenth and fifteenth centuries, and there are some very clear differences between the twelfth and thirteenth centuries and the late Middle Ages.

The mood of the fourteenth century changes from that of the thirteenth. It becomes more somber and pessimistic. From 1305 to 1378 the papacy is the captive of France and the pope lives in Avignon. From 1378 to 1418 the papacy has as many as four contenders. England experienced two incompetent kings, Edward II and Richard II, during the fourteenth century. From 1337 to 1453 England and France are locked in a brutal and draining conflict, the Hundred Years War. This is followed by the War of the Roses in England, settled only with the victory of Henry VII. The Black Death swept western Europe in the mid-fourteenth century, wiping out a good portion of the population. Following William of Ockham (d. 1349) intellectual sterility and scepticism rules in the universities, leaving theology in a shambles and opening spirituality to all kinds of excesses. It was not a good time, and the greed of the fifteenth-century papacy and the immorality of the clergy hardly helped.

However, it was also a time of heroic Christian witness. It is to this that we will largely refer in exploring the spirituality of this period.

The Rhineland Mystics

Dominican spirituality took on a new emphasis with its fourteenth-century development in the Lowlands, at the lower Rhine River. The thirteenth century had been a time for the growth of spiritual association among the laity. Particularly in the Low countries and northern France certain groups formed, called the Beguines (who lived together in houses) and the Beghards (who lived in their own homes). They practiced a form of spiritual discipline together and supported themselves by crafts. In an age where heresy was looked for under every bed they soon became suspect. Both the Beguines and the Beghards were subject more than anything else to quietism (i.e., one does not need to seek salvation, but wait for it passively).

Two mystical movements developed in this climate. First, out of the Beguines came an approach to the spiritual life, of which Beatrice of Nazareth (d. 1268) and Hadewijch of Antwerp (her writings, *Spiritual Poems,* date from 1250) are the principal exponents, called "bridal mysticism" (*Brautmystik*). It depended upon the imagery of the *Canticle,* particularly as interpreted by Bernard, and was heavily affective.

Second, there is in the writings of an anonymous author, who was also a Beguine and who is sometimes confused with Hadewijch or is called the "second Hadewijch," an approach known as the "spirituality of essence" (*Wesenmystik*). This author appears to have been influenced by Meister Eckhart. Here the image of spiritual nakedness appears. The movement is much more speculative than *Brautmystik.*

Both *Wesenmystik* and *Brautmystik* are based on the Neo-Platonic image of creation as the emanation from God, and salvation as the return of humanity or the ascent of humankind to the One from which we came. The nature of that ascent in *Wesenmystik* is related to the affinity of the human essence to the divine essence. The soul is absorbed in the essence of God. In *Brautmystik* the imagery, drawing upon Bernard and the Song of Songs, is of love and marriage. To be whole is to experience marriage with the Lamb.

The fourteenth century was a time when spiritual direction became mechanical and uninspired. Tauler, whom we shall describe shortly, complains that spiritual directors are often like hunting dogs that eat the hare instead of bringing it to their master.

(Tauler, like many medieval authors, loved hunting illustrations.)

This latter speculation pointed to the father of Rhineland mysticism, the Dominican MEISTER ECKHART (1260–1327). Extremely apophatic and speculative, the major intellectual influences of Eckhart were Aquinas, Augustine, and Dionysius. He was widely read, however, and knew the Neo-Platonists and Plato, although he was more a follower of Aristotle. He had read the Fathers as well as his near contemporaries.

God is ineffable for Eckhart; he is incomprehensible: the "superessential intellect." To know God one must enter into "the darkness of unknowing." Eckhart affirms the negative theology of Dionysius. As Augustine says, "Though we can know that God is, we cannot know what God is." Eckhart says, "Nobody is God." His notion of God is more the Neo-Platonic One than the Trinity.

Strongly given to Aquinas' intellectualism, the highest part of the soul is intellectual in essence. The intellect has a power or *spark,* called the "ground of the soul" or *scintilla animae,* which is uncreated and uncreatable. (Eckhart did not "invent" the spark as the highest part of the soul. It was a common medieval notion. For example, in Bonaventure the spark is the natural inclination to good in humanity.) The spark for Eckhart is in humanity, but is equal to God. It is the seat of the divine life, and the birth of the Word takes place here. Once that has happened there is an "identity" between the soul and God. As Eckhart says, "My truest I is God." God is all encompassing, and as we know him as such we become identified with him. But there is a distinction between God and ourselves. Eckhart is not a pantheist, although he has been and can be read that way. He also seems to have been influenced by or shared an influence with the Jewish *Kabbalah,* which also can appear to be pantheistic.

JOHN TAULER (c. 1300–1361) a Dominican, was Eckhart's most apt pupil and has been much wider read than Eckhart. He was in the tradition of *Wesenmystik,* despite the condemnation of his master (whom he was careful not to mention too frequently in his sermons). Tauler, with Eckhart, goes beyond images and concepts to the divine abyss. He dwells on the tripartite definition of the person and insists that by practicing virtue and intelligence God will dwell in the spirit by the power of God's grace. Yet when a person is in union with God he knows he is not God. The way to holiness is by reflection on the passion of Christ.

Tauler is more practical than Eckhart. He was a preacher, a pastor, and an administrator. His preaching must be seen in the light of his experience of ministering during the horror of the Black Death.

Tauler is a very important master of the spiritual life, about whom we need to know more and about whom little is accessible. He appears to be one of those pivotal persons, perhaps neglected because he is "lumped" with Eckhart, whose impact on subsequent centuries was generally either esoteric or negative. (Eckhart is usually the prototypical mystic quoted by those who wish to argue that mysticism and Christianity are incompatible.) Yet Tauler's sermons, much loved by Luther and by many who followed the German reformer, have had an influence on the mainstream of Christian spirituality for which he has been given little credit. However, we must be careful not to "Protestantize" Tauler. He was a faithful Catholic.

Particularly important for an understanding of Tauler was his relationship with Nicolas of Basle, who was the leader of the "Friends of God." This was a lay movement of persons seeking something "more" in the religious life. Tauler experienced a conversion under the influence of Nicolas, who then became his spiritual director. Nicolas gave Tauler certain "golden ABCs" of the Christian life. We get a flavor of this concrete spirituality in such items as "keep the middle path with moderation," "ponder the past with sincere repentance," "give absolution to all who have wronged you," "conquer sloth with vigour," and "be at peace with God and His creations."

What strikes the reader of Tauler is that he sounds so much more contemporary than, say, Richard of St. Victor or Bonaventure. His focus is on sin and our unworthiness. "A truly converted Christian man," he writes, "abides in sincere and humble confession of his nothingness." Sin is for Tauler self-will. For those who would claim that mystical theology has no sense of sin Tauler stands as a clear contradiction.

Prayer for Tauler is the contemplation of God. Verbal prayer is but the clothing, not the "person of prayer." The essence of prayer "is that the heart and mind go out to God without intermediary . . . the lifting up of the mind to God in love."

One is struck by Tauler's rich imagery. For example, here he plays upon the image of the wilderness.

> There are three reasons why a spiritual life is called a wilderness, or a life in the desert. The first is on account of the small number who do turn from the world and go forth into it. . . . Again, a spiritual life may fitly be called a wilderness, by reason of the many sweet flowers which spring up and flourish where they are not trodden under foot by man. . . . A third likeness . . . is that we find in the wilderness so little provision for the flesh.

But the wilderness for Tauler has the potential of both good and evil. It can be a place of vanity as well as a place where earthly care and passions are laid to rest.

In speaking of the conflict between the inner and outer man, Tauler writes,

> To the man who does not obey the strivings of God's spirit, nor experience this inward conflict, Jesus does not enter in. For all those who have never felt . . . God's heavy hand on their soul, and truly yielded to it in their life, those will never bring any good to pass so long as they live.

Tauler does not teach that we gain salvation by our efforts or that there is a "treasury of merit." One cannot do any good without first answering the call of God. Humanity is united to God by surrendering itself to the Cross of Christ.

That we may thus be nailed with Christ to the cross of his humanity, that we may be admitted to the eternal behold- ing of the brightness of His godhead, may the Almighty Trinity grant and help us.

HENRY SUSO (c. 1295–1366), a Dominican, was a practitioner of what Eckhart and Tauler wrote: mysticism. (Tauler may have had mystical experiences.) His book, *Little Book of Divine Truth,* is a very discreet and beautiful exposition of Eckhart and Tauler, as well as Suso's own personal discoveries. The stripping of the self, the union with the One, the "eternal nothingness," etc., are all there. Suso is rather naïve, going heavily into demons. But this was the spirit of his times, and the Black Death seemed to make one believe very much in the demonic. He is not a theo- logian.

In his early life Suso characterizes for us the excessive mor- tification of the flesh typical of Dominican medieval piety. It is this we often recall when we think of fourteenth- and fifteenth- century mysticism. In the Dominican convent of St. Mark, in Florence, the famous frescos of Fra Angelico (1387–1455), him- self a Dominican, are to be found in the cells of the friars on the upper level. What they show is what transpired in those cells and there is not a one in which blood is not shed through flagellation. It is to Suso's credit that he heard God telling him to do away with all that and so he threw the instruments of self-torture into the Rhine.

JOHN RUYSBROECK (1293–1381) was not a Dominican but an Augustinian, as was Luther. But he was influenced by Eckhart, as well as directly by Dionysius and also the "second Hadewijch." He did not live in the Rhineland, but he belongs to this school. He was Flemish or, in contemporary terms, Belgian. Ruysbroeck is considered by some to be both a superior theologian to Eckhart and to have experienced what he wrote (Eckhart was not a mys- tic). His influence on later centuries is comparable to that of Tauler. He is more balanced than Eckhart and clearly avoids pantheism. In later life Ruysbroeck is hesitant to assert the possibility of an intuitive vision of the divine essence, which is a backing away from the excesses of Eckhart.

He is an interesting and thoughtful expositor of *exemplarism*. This theory holds that the expansion and return with the life of the Holy Trinity is shared by the creature. The soul is modelled on the divine pattern: memory, understanding, and will. Remember William of St. Thierry and Lull and look forward to Ignatius Loyola. Yet the soul is one. It is a three-in-one. Man therefore comes to understand God by understanding himself. This notion appears in *The Cloud of Unknowing,* whose author was a contemporary of Ruysbroeck. The exemplarism of Ruysbroeck is in the tradition of *Wesenmystik.*

Instrumental Images
  The spark, *scintilla animae.*
  Brautmystik.
  Wesenmystik.
  Exemplarism.

Terminal Images
  Identity—"My truest I is God."
  The knowledge of the inner self.

SELECT BIBLIOGRAPHY
Meister Eckhart, *A Modern Translation,* translated by Raymond B. Bla. Harper, 1941.
———, *Parisian Questions and Prologues,* translated by Armand A. Maurer. Pontifical Institute, 1974.
———, *Treatises and Sermons,* translated by James M. Clark and John V. Skinnner. Harper, 1958.
Henry Suso, *The Exemplar,* translated by Mary Ann Edward. Allenson, 1962.
John Ruysbroeck, *The Chastening of God's Children and the Treatise of Perfection of the Sons of God,* translated by Eric Colledge and Joyce Bazire. Allenson, 1957.

John Tauler, *Spiritual Conferences,* translated by Eric Colledge and Sr. M. Janes. Christian Classics, 1961.

The English Mystics

As the fourteenth century unfolded and the sociopolitical situation in Western Europe degenerated it is, perhaps, no surprise that it was a time when many people reported visions, ecstasies, and private revelations. They are the kind of phenomena which seem to accompany social unrest or uncertainty; although one must be hesitant in writing off all such visions as "wishful thinking."

The fourteenth-century English mystics run the gamut from apophatic to kataphatic. They tend to be affective, since the English mind is not given to abstract thought. Martin Thornton argues that the English mystics produce a synthesis of the speculative/affective. It may just be fuzzy thinking. One interesting thing about the fourteenth-century English mystics is that they are all in some sense an expression of the anchorite movement—an anchorite now being someone living in a cell attached to a parish church. The anchorite served as a spiritual director. The *Ancren Riwle,* "The Anchoress' Rule," written at the beginning of the thirteenth century in Middle English had a profound influence upon subsequent treatises in the fourteenth century and, at the same time, is indicative of the anchorite bias of pre-Reformation English spirituality. It was a "masterpiece of religious guidance unrivaled for almost two centuries." At the same time, however, it lacks theological clarity.

RICHARD ROLLE (c. 1295–1349) was probably a disaffected theologian who became a hermit—different from an anchorite in that he wandered—after finishing his studies at the Sorbonne in Paris and returning to England. He is contemptuous of abstract thought but deeply steeped in the Scriptures. The whole anti-intellectual spirit of the fourteenth century is summed up in Rolle's comment,

> An old woman can be more expert in the love of God—and
> less worldly too—than your theologian with his useless study-
> ing. He does it for vanity, to get a reputation, to obtain
> stipends and official positions. Such a fellow ought to be en-
> titled not 'Doctor' but 'Fool.'

Rolle's fear of women, including his sister, is a familiar theme
in Christian spirituality by this time. What he says appears to
contradict what he attributes to theologians. Women, he tells us,
are deficient in reason and, therefore, "are much in need of the
counsel of good men." But one must be cautious. "No neglect of
his soul is more damnable than that of the man who looks after a
woman to lust after her."

Rolle writes eloquently in both English and Latin, which
makes him one of the first authors to write in Middle English
(Chaucer is a half-century later). Three images dominate his writings. First, the fire of love, which has nothing to do with fraternal love, pertains to a mystical love that comes at the height of
comtemplation. This was found also in John Cassian 900 years
before. Second, his use of the mystical image of the "song of
love" (*melos amores*), experienced in union with God, is striking.
Third, heat (*calor*) is something to which he testifies and that is
well known in psychological studies of mysticism. Heat appears
in Paschel's description of ecstasy, and is found in contemporary
accounts of mystical experience. He speaks of rapture and sweetness, notions that have become common to the kataphatic and affective contemplatives; but they are not just sentimental. There is
a real sensibility in Rolle. He is "heroic." He warns against the
temptations of those who "are led astray by the *demons of the noonday Sun* into a sham and fanciful devotion." The tendency of
Anglician spirituality to lapse into "moderation"—like the
church at Laodicea (Rev. 3:15)—in honor of synthesis and balance is totally absent in Rolle. For this we can give thanks.

Rolle makes reference to the *"inner eye."*

> From the time my conversion of life and mind began until the
> day the door of Heaven swung back and his Face was re-

vealed, so that my inner eye could contemplate the things
that are above, and see by what way it might find the Beloved
and cling to him, three years passed.

Julian of Norwich mentions her "spiritual eye." Here we have the
Western emphasis on vision—seeing God's face—with an ana-
tomical metaphor: an inner or spiritual eye (although it also is
found in the pseudo-Macarius). In primitive cultures the *shaman*
was said to have a "third eye" which enabled him to see the
spirits. It seems to be a reference to a particular experience, similar to what psychologists mean when they say they "hear with a
third ear"—meaning they record their inner reactions to the presence and words of the client. It may also refer to the same thing
that Carlos Castaneda mentions when he describes seeing as opposed to looking.

Rolle is in the Western medieval tradition of Gregory the
Great, Bernard, and Richard of St. Victor.

The Cloud of Unknowing, written by an unknown Midland
priest about 1370, is a gem of fourteenth-century spirituality.
One of its purposes is to correct Rolle. The author is apophatic,
but affective. It is not *gnōsis* that the contemplative seeks, but
love. "Only to our intellect is he [God] incomprehensible: not to
our love." He is principally indebted to Richard of St. Victor, or
possibly Thomas Gallus of St. Victor, but also to Augustine and
Dionysius. "It is quite right that in contemplation God should be
loved for himself alone above all created things, for as we have
said already, this work is fundamentally a naked intent, none
other than the singleminded intention of our spirit directed to
God himself alone. . . . By 'darkness' I mean 'a lack of knowing'. . . . For this reason it is called a 'cloud,' not of the sky, of
course, but 'of unknowing,' a cloud of unknowing between you
and your God." The "cloud" is a type of poverty. His teaching
also had a certain affinity to John of the Cross.

The author also shares the exemplarism of the Rhineland mystics, as does Walter Hilton. "Therefore strain every nerve in every
possible way to know and experience yourself as you really are. It

will not be long, I suspect, before you have a real knowledge and experience of God as he is." He also subscribes with the Rhineland mystics to the *scintilla animae* or *scintilla synderesis*. (*Synderesis* is the working together of will and intellect.)

I would note in passing that Martin Thornton, writing on English spirituality in 1963, does not devote anything more than a sentence or two to *The Cloud of Unknowing*. Fifteen years later there seems little doubt that of all the fourteenth-century English mystics the unknown author of the spiritual classic is the most widely read.

JULIAN OF NORWICH (Feast day: May 8) described her visions of 1373. She is highly kataphatic and affective. She is enjoying particular popularity today because of her references to God as our mother—something that has in the past been the cause of shock and has even been expurgated from editions of her writings. "So Jesus Christ, who opposes good to evil, is our true mother." Actually there is ample precedent for this devotion in medieval authors—particularly in English sources. Julian stands in the tradition of Bernard, William of St. Thierry, the Victorines, Anselm, and Aquinas. She is optimistic, exuding a Benedictine warmth. God greatly rejoices in humanity's fall "for raising on high and fulness of bliss which mankind has come to, exceeding what we should have if he had not fallen." There are the well-known words to her from Jesus, which T. S. Eliot quotes in "Four Quartets": "Sin must needs be, but all shall be well. All shall be well; and all manner of thing shall be well."

Julian is christocentric. She embraces the Cross and this keeps her from being sentimental. Her interest in the Passion is quite Franciscan in spirit. She is deeply eucharistic, and sees prayer always against the background of the worship of the church (contrary to Evelyn Underhill's erroneous judgment). "A sure thing it is, a good and a gracious, to will, meekly and mightily, to be fastened and oned to our Mother Holy Church; that is, Christ Jesus."

Prayer is not a formal exercise for Julian, but an act of habitual recollection—an idea that also appears in Walter Hilton—which is an English form of the constant prayer of the Desert Fathers. "Prayer oneth the soul of God . . . prayer is a witness that the soul willeth as God willeth, it . . . enableth him to receive grace. . . . All our intent and all our might is set wholly upon this beholding of him (Jesus). And this is high and ineffable prayer as I see it. . . . It is thus that we may, with his sweet grace in our own need, continual prayer, come into him now."

Julian had visions, which bothers some people. Yet she is remarkably tempered for her times, since many self-appointed "mystics" in that era were given to tales of visitation by demons, as well as saints and God himself. She also says some things that are not impeccably orthodox, which concerns others. But she is a passionate woman, preeminently Anglician in spirit. She understands what Gregory of Nyssa means by perfection. The spiritual life is not a matter of "being saved," but "the soul's constant search pleases God greatly." With William of St. Thierry Dame Julian believes that "in every soul which will be saved there is a godly will which never assents to sin and never will." She obviously follows the exemplarism of the author of *The Cloud of Unknowing*. "And when we know and see, truly and clearly, what our self is, then we shall truly and clearly see and know our Lord God in the fulness of joy."

WALTER HILTON (c. 1396), an Augustinian canon, wrote the *Scale of Perfection*—the "scale" being a ladder. He had obviously read Rolle and *The Cloud of Unknowing*, correcting the latter's corrections of the former. This work is a relatively systematic treatise on the spiritual life as seen by an English Augustinian. Hilton had spiritual guides in mind as readers. His book is rather unexceptional in its ideas. He deals with a problem with which medieval persons struggle mightily. The problem was the "Mary and Martha issue"—an image taken from Augustine of the two roles of the Christian disciple: active and contemplative. Hilton works hard in this book to show how one can be a contemplative in the active state. He is kataphatic and affective, although there are some apophatic elements. Martin Thornton considers him the primary, fundamental source for understanding English spirituality. He shares with Julian an advocacy of *habitual recollection* and, with the author of the *Cloud*, the belief that love is the experience of union with God.

MARGERY KEMPE (c. 1373–after 1433) wrote the *Book of Margery Kempe*, which was lost until 1934. Some, like Dom Francois Vanderbroucke, think her psychotic—she certainly went mad for a while—and some, like Martin Thornton, think she is great. She herself described the revulsion some feel in her writing. Julian of Norwich, her spiritual director, assured her she was not possessed. She was married, had fourteen children, and then took a vow of chastity with her husband (as well she might, after fourteen children!). She is christocentric—much involved with the Passion—and gives a highly symbolic exegesis of habitual recollection. She loved pilgrimages. She had many visions and had the gift of tears. Like the Victorines, she was very much given to seeing the extraordinary in the ordinary, which in her case might lead one to think she was a bit "spooky."

Instrumental Images
   Habitual recollection.
   Inner or Spiritual eye.

Terminal Images
   Song of love.
   Heat.
   Motherhood of God.

SELECT BIBLIOGRAPHY
The Cloud of Unknowing, edited by William Johnston. Doubleday, 1973.
Walter Hilton, *The Scale of Perfection*, edited by L. Sherley-Price. Penguin, 1957.
Julian of Norwich, *Showings*, translated by Edmond Colledge and James Walsh. Paulist Press, 1978.

Margery B. Kempe, *Book of,* edited by Sanford B. Meech. Oxford, 1940.

Richard Rolle, *English Writings,* Somerset, 1931.

————, *The Fire of Love and the Mending of Life,* translated by Richard Misyn. Kraus reprints, n.d.

————, *Selected Writings,* translated by John G. Harrell. SPCK, 1963.

The Fifteenth-Century Demise

Pietism is a term which, while historically rooted to the late seventeenth century, describes a degeneration of spirituality that may be characterized more generally as suffering from sentimentality, biblicism, personalism, exclusionism, fideism, anti-intellectualism, etc. It flourishes in self-congratulatory small groups. It is impervious to criticism because it recognizes no canon of truth outside the subjective meaning of its membership.

This may be because pietism is over against a kind of thinking which is *differentiated.* Differentiated thinking is not "primitive" in the sense of Levy Bruehl's "primitive mystique." It separates things from the names for things; and, as in nominalism, may even deny the reality of the relationship of things or, as in idealism, the things themselves. Differentiated thinking is a product of the twelfth and thirteenth centuries. It was not common to humanity in the Heroic Age, where magic combined with deep sensibility. No one could rightly accuse ninth-century people of being sentimental. That is not true of fifteenth-century people. Pietism is excessively kataphatic and affective to the point of being repulsive. Whereas there is no doubt that elements of pietism existed before the fifteenth century, it rears its ugly head there most clearly for the first time.

The fifteenth century is also a time when an increasing preoccupation with the occult, particularly witches, takes place. From 1427, when publication of discourses on witchcraft began to proliferate, until 1486 and the publication of the notorious *Malleus Maleficarum,* the whole phenomenon took on a developed form. Some believe that the belief in witches, which prevails through-

out human history in many cultures, is related to a collapse of a
sense of individual integrity and the possibility of personal
achievement. Evil, over which we seem to have no control, is attributed to outside forces and we become corporately paranoid. It
would be interesting to explore the relationship between pietism
and witchcraft.

A Dutchman, GERARD GROOTE (1340–1384)—an acquaint-
ance of Ruysbroeck but not a disciple—gave birth to the *Devotio
moderna,* which is a form of pietism. In England the last of the
late medieval mystics, Margery Kempe, wrote in an excessive
manner which gave encouragement to extravagently affective
prayer. Pietism is always a reaction to disappointing and sterile
theology—German Protestant scholasticism in the late seventeenth century, the rise of scientific positivism in the mid-nine-
teenth century, the radical theology of the 1960s, and the cyni-
cism generated by nominalism in the fifteenth century.

Groote and his followers taught a spirituality which was pessimistic and practical. They were obsessed with the seeming de-
bauchery of the clergy and the apparent pantheism of the mystics.
They advocated conversion of the heart, the practice of virtue, the
endurance of trials, the apostolate, and, above all, eternal salvation. Action and contemplation were to them the same thing,
and there is very little notion of a process of spiritual growth. All
depended upon the imitation of the humanity of Jesus. These are
all themes which will recur in pietism from the fifteenth century
to the present date.

Thomas Merton makes the following important observations
about the *Devotio moderna,* which generally applies to pietism in
all centuries. The *Devotio moderna* insists on the personal devotion
to the humanity of Christ and highly affective prayer. This is the
result, at least in part, of a reaction to the mysticism of persons
such as Eckhart and Tauler. It has the effect, however, of divorc-
ing personal prayer from liturgical prayer—a separation totally
unknown to the piety of the High Middle Ages but certainly
characteristic of pietism today. On this basis, Merton claims, we

will discover, when we move into the sixteenth century, that spiritual renewal consisted of a preoccupation with personal devotion which never touched liturgical prayer. (The liturgy, while sterile, seemed to function on its own.) Second- and third-rate spiritual directors will make "method" an end, not a means, and an image of the spiritual director as tyrant will arise, against which the protests of the true masters—e.g., Dom Augustine Baker of England—will not be heard.

An example of fifteenth-century piety that particularly needs to be remembered is the *Imitation of Christ* by THOMAS À KEMPIS (c. 1380–1571; Feast day: July 24), a Dutchman. The book is misnamed. It is really not devoted to the ascetical practice of the imitation of Christ, although it is principally a treatise on instrumental or ascetial images rather than terminal or mystical images. The major theme is the interior life and the Eucharist. The author is skeptical as to the possibility of the vision of God, particularly in God's essence. He embodies that curious sharp division between nature and supernature and embraces antirationalism, both of which are characteristic of pietism.

His style is aphoristic. For example, on the separation of nature and supernature, Thomas à Kempis writes, "He that esteemeth himself viler than all men, and judgeth himself most unworthy, is fittest to receive the greater blessings." His antirationalism is implied in this statement: "He made greater progress by forsaking all things, than by studying subtle niceties." This is reminiscent of Richard Rolle. The following is a bit more on target. "Jesus had now many lovers of his heavenly kingdom, but few bearers of his Cross." Another statement, however—"Blessed is he that understandeth what it is to love Jesus, and to despise himself for Jesus' sake."—casts it in a more gloomy light.

The impact of this book on subsequent centuries, including Martin Luther, has been immense. Since it is not spiritual writing of particularly high quality, this is to be regretted.

Two other persons need to be mentioned before we leave the

fifteenth century, John Gerson and Catherine of Genoa. They are very different witnesses to the piety of this period. The first person of importance, if for no other reason than his impact on John Calvin, is JOHN GERSON (1363–1429), chancellor of the University of Paris and a principal leader at the Council of Constance (1414–1418). There are, in fact, also some other very important reasons for noting Gerson. He was an intellectual, but a throwback to the pre-fourteenth-century Dionysian school (e.g., as in the Victorines and Bonaventure). What he has most in common with the *Devotio moderna* is the suspicion of the extravagant speculations of the Dominican mystics of the fourteenth century. He believed that mystical knowledge was experimental. The *Devotio moderna* made a profound impact upon French humanism in the fifteenth century and, since he was in many ways the central figure in French humanism, he is certainly important to the *Devotio moderna*. But Gerson did not, of course, accept the anti-intellectualism of that movement.

What is particularly fascinating about Gerson is his approach to the ascent of God. There is a necessary condition (or a pre-condition) to this ascent—repentance, and then six steps. The six steps are not necessarily in sequence, however. There are three steps in the speculative domain: simple intelligence, reason, and contemplation. They seem to bear some relationship to Richard of St. Victor's imagination, reason, and understanding; although imagination plays a role in contemplation, something like Owen Barfield's "final participation" in *Saving the Appearances* or Paul Ricouer's "second naïvete" in *The Symbolism of Evil*. There are also three steps in the affective domain: the animal appetite (passion), the rational appetite (devotion), and the supernatural appetite (love). The speculative domain opens one to the love of God, or a person may proceed through the three steps of the affective domain without going through the rational. In this way, in the spirit of the *Devotio moderna*, Gerson preserves the mystical experience for the ordinary person.

But the intellect is also necessary for the evaluation of the claim to have experienced God. Gerson will not accept the testimony of even ordinary persons to the vision of God on the basis of their feelings alone. Their testimony must appear reasonable, which, of course, sets him off from the main stream of pietism, as well as quietism, both of which arise in the fifteenth century.

What Gerson wanted to do was join theology and piety. He believed that the renewal of the church required a deep spiritual awakening, and that could only come about through the interrelation of cognition and the interior life. He revived the ancient word *pietas,* which in the medieval world had given place to *devotio* (as we saw in Bernard), and after which the *Devotio moderna* is named. *Devotio* means total dedication, and the *Devotio moderna* means dedication to the affective experience. The emergence of the *Devotio moderna* signaled the breakdown of the unity between theology and spirituality. By introducing the notion of *pietas,* Gerson hoped to join wisdom to affect and to call for a spirituality that took the internal life seriously. He believed himself to be indebted to Augustine and Bonaventure for this use of *pietas.*

The second person of note in the fifteenth century, whom Evelyn Underhill described as the only first-rate spiritual genius of her time, was CATHERINE OF GENOA (1447–1510). Like Gerson, Catherine was both a product of her times and yet rose above the mawkish and superstitious piety characteristic of the late fifteenth century. From adolescence, she was given to deep devotion. The story of her life reveals a person who overcame depression and personal struggle to achieve a high degree of integration and authenticity.

Catherine was the daughter of an Italian noble family. She was married to an unfaithful husband, whom she later converted. She herself underwent a profound conversion experience, which led to her serving in a hospital for the poor of Genoa for the rest of her life. There is in Catherine a combination of severe abnegation and mortification, with accompanying mystical phenomena admired at this time, and a profound social concern. While some writers have suggested she was a quietist, this hardly seems consistent with her work among the poor. Catherine was instrumental in the founding of the Oratory of Divine Love, which had a great influence on the Roman Catholic reformation in Italy in the sixteenth century.

Catherine's principal teaching concerns itself with the spiritual combat between the pure love of God and the self love of humanity. There is a definite Dionysian element in Catherine's teaching as well as an Augustinian and Franciscan tone. Unlike Synesius, for example, Catherine does not believe that "created things" are a means of knowing the divine. With John of the Cross in the next century, she says our senses fail us. Catherine transcends the anti-mystical spirit of *Devotio moderna* and serves as a bridge for the Italian church between fourteenth and sixteenth century mysticism. Her influence in later centuries knows no denominational boundaries. She had a strong influence on Frederich von Hügel and others in the nineteenth century.

The problem with the fifteenth century and those who imitated it is that they appreciated neither Gerson and his struggle to unite theology and piety nor Catherine's social witness, in spite of the appearance of excessive piety. Gerson's struggle for the unity of theology and piety remains a goal, along with the struggle to reconcile the private life and public world of Christians. Pietism of subsequent times followed all that was bad in the *Devotio moderna,* and ignored the good which Gerson sought to evoke in the concept of *pietas.*

SELECT BIBLIOGRAPHY
Catherine of Genoa, *Purgation and Purgatory, Spiritual Dialogue,* translated by Serge Hughes, Paulist Press, 1979.
Thomas à Kempis, *Imitation of Christ,* Dutton, 1976.

·III·

Byzantine Spirituality

A brief note is necessary here to bring up a few names and images essential to the history of Christian spirituality from the church in the East. Relatively untouched by the Germanic invasions of the fifth century, the new Rome survived at Constantinople——previously Byzantium, now Istanbul——until its fall to the Muslims in 1453. We have to keep in mind the permanent breach between the churches of the East and the West from 1054, although schism existed before that. The Byzantine Empire survived for almost 1000 years.

We left the East with the seventh century, John Climacus, and Maximus the Confessor. Both of these men stand in the tradition of Gregory of Nyssa and Evagrius. Maximus turns Evagrius upside down, however, and makes faith the summit of the spiritual quest and not the base. Practice must accompany contemplation. He is thoroughly biblical and Christian. He also teaches that because God is an infinite abyss, he is eminently mysterious. Finally, God fulfills by his "divine operation" our human *energia*. *Energia* is a Greek word meaning "that which works in us". This is a repeat of the whole concept of *synergy*. It happens as the Logos of God lights up the Logos that is in the *nous* of man.

John Climacus is a teacher of asceticism as Maximus is of mysticism. Both he and Maximus shape future Byzantine spirituality. John is made of stern stuff. He tell us we must meditate upon our own death as the most useful of all spiritual practices. The spiritual ascent is an act of dying.

Byzantine spirituality was deeply monastic. The two great monastic centers at the height of the Byzantine Empire were the monastery of St. Catherine on Mt. Sinai, where John Climacus was abbot, and the monastery at Constantinople, where Maximus lived. The monasticism on Mt. Sinai—called Sinaitic monasticism—was both austere and charismatic (Hesychasm, particularly as related to breathing and the Jesus Prayer, comes out of Sinai.) The monasticism at Constantinople, called Studite monasticism after a monastic official of the fifth century, was active and involved. The tension between Sinaitic and Studite monasticism was one of the most creative such tensions in Byzantine spirituality.

The interaction between Sinaitic and Studite monasticism found particular form in SIMEON THE NEW THEOLOGIAN (949–1022). Simeon made a great deal out of the leadership of the mystics or "spirituals" as against that of the ecclesiastical hierarchy, which got him into trouble. Simeon's approach was grounded in the Byzantine concept of "deification" as the height and ultimate goal of contemplation. He taught that the Holy Spirit comes as a sudden transforming experience. He believed that mystical illumination is normative in the authentic Christian life. The presence of the Spirit is, however, a gift of grace. If one is to teach, be he priest or bishop, about the Spirit, he cannot do it unless he manifests in his life that Presence. Simeon believed that consciousness of the Spirit was accompanied by obedience to the commandments.

The presence of the Spirit manifests itself in fraternal love. Simeon is very clear about this. There is nothing pantheistic about his mysticism, but rather it bespeaks a dialogue with Christ resulting in both compunction and tears. The *vision of light* and *tears* are characteristic of Simeon's mysticism.

It needs to be noted here in passing that the Byzantine liturgy and inconography are extremely important. The Studite tradition brought in from Syria much of what we identify with the Byzantine liturgy and iconography. The principle that lies within Byzantine liturgy and inconography is that of the symbol, which veils what is invisible and eternal. The liturgy and its setting are a kind of incarnation. The church is heaven on earth. The cupola, particularly with the *Christos Pantokrator* at the apex, is the heavenly church. In our participation we become members of the choir of the saints, anticipating our deification. The icons are windows—paintings to be interpreted at a deeper level—into the mystery of God.

In the tenth century a new monastic tradition began to evolve on Mt. Athos in Greece. As it developed it gave full form to hesychasm and the Jesus Prayer. No longer was prayer centered in the mind or *nous,* the identification of the Logos of the person with the Logos of God. The idea was to get the mind into the heart, and so the prayer of the heart becomes the rule. (This must not be confused with contemporary reference to affective prayer as "of the heart.") Keep in mind the distinction we noted between the pseudo-Macarius and Evagrius. The search for calm, the unwearying repeating of the Jesus Prayer, holding the breath, and, gazing fixedly at one's navel become the accepted method for getting the mind into the heart.

GREGORY PALAMAS (c. 1296–1359) was the last great Byzantine spiritual master. He was trained at Mt. Athos in hesychasm and became its chief exponent. He described the heart as the storehouse of our thoughts, and advocated the Jesus Prayer. He engaged in a famous controversy with a Platonist-turned-Nominalist, Barlaam, who ridiculed the hesychasts on the grounds that they claimed to see the essence of God. Gregory Palamas, in the tradition of Gregory of Nyssa, argued that we do not see the essence but the "uncreated light" of the divine energies (*energia*). This energy is uncreated; it enables us to participate in God. This is the same light which Peter, James, and John saw on Mt. Tabor at the Transfiguration of Jesus, so the Eastern church calls it *Taboric light.* The Taboric light is a kind of *Shekin-*

ah: the goal of the spiritual life. The process of spiritual growth is the removal of scales from our eyes that we might see the light. Consequently purgation and illumination go on at the same time.

Instrumental Images
   Holding of breath and navel-gazing.

Terminal Images
   Divine energies.
   Taboric light.
   Consciousness of the Spirit.

SELECT BIBLIOGRAPHY

Early Fathers from the Philokalia: Together with Some Writings of St. Abba Dorotheus, St. Isaac of Syria and St. Gregory Palamas, translated by E. Kadloubovsky and G. E. H. Palmer. Faber and Faber, 1954.

Writings from the Philokalia on Prayer of the Heart, translated by E. Kadloubovsky and G. E. H. Palmer. Faber and Faber, 1951.

·IV·

The Modern Period

The Spanish School

The sixteenth century is, more than anything else, when reason drives out all else. We become obsessed with logic, analysis, and explanation. This brought many gifts and lost us much. As a consequence, however, we get *the first science of the spiritual life,* beginning with three great Spanish spiritual masters: IGNATIUS LOYOLA (1491 or 1495–1556), TERESA OF AVILA (1515–1582), and JOHN OF THE CROSS (1542–1591). Ignatius was the founder of the Jesuits, the latter two were reformers of the Carmelites. The Carmelites are an order founded in the twelfth century in Palestine during the Crusades. Its first house was on Mt. Carmel, where St. Mary was reputed to have been assumed into heaven and where the prophet Elijah slew the prophets of Baal. Scientific spirituality means a systematic analysis of the totality of the spiritual experience with the intention of describing both the means and ends of that experience in such a way that it can be taught and followed, as well as compared with other systems.

The precursor of sixteenth-century Spanish spirituality was a talented man, GARCIA XIMENES DE CISNEROS (1475–1510). He wrote a book entitled *The Spiritual Exercises,* which heralded the more famous treatise of the same name. He represented a late medieval interest in the methodology of meditation developed among the Franciscans and the leaders of the *Devotio moderna.*

Ignatius was born of a noble family, whose castle was Loyola. He was a soldier until in 1521 when at the siege of Pampeluna a cannon ball passed between his legs, wounding him. During his recovery he underwent a profound change in his life and, having hung his sword in the Lady Chapel at Montserrat, went "on retreat" to Manresa. The Society of Jesus was the result of a group of six young men Ignatius gathered around him while he studied for the priesthood in Paris, 1528–1535. They first called themselves "the companions of Jesus." The society itself was founded in 1539, with the drawing up of the so-called "Deliberation of the First Fathers." *The Spiritual Exercises* are really Ignatius' notes in leading other individuals to an openness to the experience of God. They are ascetical outlines for directors (unlike Ximenez's work, which was aimed at the directees). "Spiritual Exercises" (a phrase that goes back many centuries in Christian spirituality) are what Ignatius called his retreats. His book is therefore entitled *Spiritual Exercises,* but was not intended by him to exhaust all possible spiritual exercises or even those "Spiritual Exercises" he provided. There is great flexibility in his system.

One thing needs to be made very clear. Ignatius warns against the indiscriminate use of methods of meditation by unschooled and unguided persons. In making this warning he finds common cause with many spiritual masters—Western and Eastern—because meditative techniques without direction can trigger irreversible mental disorder or be the cause of alienation from God. The analogue would be those in contemporary times who advocate the use of LSD, but never without the presence of a guide and prior knowledge of what to expect. The deautomization of consciousness in any form—intentional or chemical—is dangerous, even while necessary.

Ignatius' motto was *Ad majorem gloriam Dei,* "To the greater glory of God." It is very reminiscent of the statements of reformed religion as to the true end of man. Ignatius was a sixteenth-century man, who believed himself to be a soldier of Christ, reforming the church wihthin, suppressing heresy, and converting the pagans. The *Exercises* trained the soldiers, but with understanding of individual needs. They also sought to assist the retreatant in making a life choice.

Ignatius takes the classical faculties of the mind—memory, understanding, and will—and treats them in a systematic manner. Memory exists to recall the sin of the fallen angels, to arouse our emotion to seek the salvation of our souls. This is the main concern of the Christian person: to save his or her soul. Understanding is the application of reason to our situation. Through our reason God illumines our world. Our will is then moved and it is joined to the will of God. Since Ignatius is concerned for the apostolate, it is the action of the will that is the supreme good.

In contemplation Ignatius tells us that we will experience both consolation and desolation. This is in accord with contemporary psychological studies which report that ecstatic experience usually involves conflicting emotion: joy and terror, bliss and sadness, and attraction and repulsion. Consolation is where love is present. It is a common word in medieval mysticism, but it will take on a special significance in late seventeenth-century pietism. Desolation is the darkness of the soul, a time of great temptation. Ignatius advises tht one never make any change of resolution when experiencing desolation.

The purpose of the *Exercises* was to enable the retreatant to be open to the same experience of God that Ignatius found at Cardoner in 1522 in a mystical vision. They are not the mechanical imposition of categories, although Ignatius' imagery, which was typical of his age, may seem to imply this. It would appear, on the contrary, that Ignatius uses the action mode of consciousness to move his readers into the receptive mode of consciousness. Ignatius was a Spaniard influenced by the romantic ideals of feudalism, who chose to be a medieval man rather than a citizen of the Reformation. Therefore, the image of Christ was very much related to the vassal-lord relationship, and he saw himself and his followers as knights errant for Christ. He is kataphatic and moderately speculative.

It is impossible to compress the teaching and significance of Ignatius into this outline, but it is important that the bare bones of his methods in prayer be provided.

First Method (for the illiterate)

I. Preparation
 1. Consider what one will do (composition of place).
 2. Pray for grace.

II. Body
   Consider a chosen subject, such as the Ten Commandments, the Commandments of the Church, the Seven Deadly Sins, the powers of the soul (memory, understanding, will), the five senses, the works of mercy. (The powers of the soul have, as we have seen, been common categories in medieval spirituality and are now in Ignatius. They reappear again and again, as, for example, in the Anglican, William Law, in the eighteenth century.)

III. Colloquy (i.e., an intimate, familiar, loving conversation such as a child has with a father)

This method is very much like an examination of one's conscience, only more. All Ignatian methods follow in some way the threefold shape of this method: preparation, body, colloquy.

Second Method (word by word)

Related to monologistic prayer but not the same thing, in the body of this method the participant reflects upon each word of a prayer, such as the Lord's Prayer.

Third Method (by way of musical measure)

This requires the association of breathing with the second method. It seeks a set rhythm. One word only is said between each breath and the participant thinks during each breath of the following:

1. The meaning of the word.
2. The person to whom one is speaking,
3. *or* the state of one's own life,
4. *or* the contrast between God and ourselves.

Fourth Method (using the five senses)

The body of this method requires that in turn we take an image—e.g., the Trial of Jesus, his Passion, the Resurrection, etc.—and apply each of the five senses to that image: sight, hearing, smell, taste, feeling.

Fifth Method (Ignatian proper)

Two things precede the preparation. Read a passage of Scripture the night before, reflect upon it, and choose one or two points for meditation. The next morning arise quickly and focus the mind on the passage and its inspiration.

I. Preparation
  1. Briefly recall the subject and points chosen.
  2. See the place, which is to imagine the scene and focus on the significant images.
  3. Pray to know, love, and follow the Lord.
II. Body
  Apply to the scene and its central images:
  1. memory, and then
  2. understanding, and finally
  3. will, so that one may act.

III. Colloquy
  Pray for grace to keep our resolutions.

Contrary to Aquinas, Ignatius seems to define meditation as simply thinking about God, and contemplation as looking at some scene from the life of Christ.

TERESA OF AVILA (sometimes described as "of Jesus") (1515–1582) was one of the greatest Christian women that ever lived. She reformed the Carmelite Order—she is considered the founder of the Order of Discalced (i.e., without shoes) Carmelites (ODC)—and was a person of great practicality. At the same time she is a remarkable mystic and teacher of the prayer life. On the whole she is kataphatic, but she possesses a remarkably balanced style of spirituality—affective and speculative, occasionally apophatic.

Her original contribution to spiritual theology was the description of the process between discursive meditation and union with God. She knew the process from her own experience. She experienced a long period of spiritual aridity and then, in 1557, had the first of a series of ecstasies, which she calls "raptures." She describes them in strongly sexual images.

She defines the degrees of prayer by means of the image of watering the garden.

1. *Discursive meditation* (the use of reason—watering bucket by bucket, carried by hand from the well).
2. *Recollection* (affective prayer)—the water wheel.
3. *Quiet*—springs of water.
4. *Union*—drenching rain.

This classification is found in her *Life.* A more developed treatment of spiritual growth is the subject of the *Interior Castle,* in which she describes seven kinds of "rooms" in the "castle" of the soul.

1. A state of grace in which we are still very much in love with the world.
2. An openness to the practice of prayer and edifying books, sermons, and conversations, while still in the world.
3. A life of high virtue, still susceptible to lapses.
4. The experience of spiritual consolations, as in the prayer of quiet.
5. A kind of incipient union.
6. A growth in intimacy with God.
7. Spiritual marriage.

The "rooms" from four to seven are the degrees of mystical experience. The last three rooms correspond to the prayer of union which Teresa describes as the drenching rain. The sign of advance in the prayer of union is a death-like experience that moves us beyond seeing, hearing, and understanding. An example would be Carlos Castaneda's vision of the coyote at the end of *The Journey to Ixtlan*. In the sixth room we find a sense of power, tranquillity, and awareness of God's word in our life as signs of the authenticity of the experience.

There has probably never been a more "healthy" Christian than Teresa. She embodies an intrinsic religious motivation. There is a balance of piety and politics, religious experience and prophetic insight, that is a witness to us all. It has been noted that there are seven elements which characterize Teresa. They are (1) trust in persons and the universe; (2) hope in the direction of history; (3) a sense of grace, or being loved for nothing, (4) an identity which is open to the new; (5) an integrity of life, which maintains a consistency between the intuitive and rational realms of consciousness; (6) a willingness to sacrifice for the public good; and (7) a vision of the future.

JOHN OF THE CROSS (1542–1591) was a cofounder with Teresa of the Discalced Carmelites. A poet, a native psychologist, a Thomistic theologian, and the mystic's mystic, he is, with Teresa, a giant in the history of Christian spirituality. He combines a number of influences: Gregory of Nyssa, Dionysius, Augustine, Bernard, Richard of St. Victor, Ruysbroeck, and even Thomas à Kempis. He is also profoundly biblical. If we "take Scripture as our guide," John says, "we do not err." In a very kataphatic and sometimes affective manner, he advocates an apophatic and speculative spirituality. From 1577 to 1578 he was imprisoned and tortured by the Carmelites of the Old Observance—to give you an idea of how seriously the issues were taken in Spain in those days. Some of his greatest writing began in his prison cell, while his habit was stuck to his back with clotted blood from beatings.

John of the Cross modifies the "three ways." They are for him *purgation*, which includes illumination within what he calls the dark night; *bethrothal;* and *spiritual marriage*. As with other six-teenth-century masters the *Brautmystik* is very strong. Union with God is a union of likeness, which harks back to the second-century distinction of Irenaeus between the image of God, which we never lose, and the likeness of God, which we must acquire. The spiritual life is a clearing of the smeared window of our soul.

It is interesting to see what John does with the three faculties of the soul. Memory and understanding are for him cognitive, and they must eventually pass. Like Gerson before him, he says that the will is appetitive, but in a supernatural manner. The dark night abolishes both inordinate appetites and cognition, but our union with God comes about through the appetitite of the will.

The ladder of ascent for John of the Cross consists of ten steps:

1. The soul becomes sick for the glory of God.
2. The soul searches for God unceasingly.
3. The soul is moved to do works for God.
4. The soul suffers, the flesh is conquered, and God gives joy.
5. The soul has an impatient desire and longing for God.
6. The soul runs swiftly toward God and senses his touch.
7. The soul acquires an ardent boldness.
8. The soul lays hold of God as the beloved.
9. The soul burns gently with love.
10. The soul is assimilated to God, apparently after death.

John of the Cross has a low estimate of people who suffer from what he calls the "spiritual sweettooth." These are individuals who like to dabble in prayer, getting an occasional "thrill," and posing as holy people. They are ascetical dilettantes, who go from one spiritual director to another, quote the latest books on prayer, and subtly boast of spiritual epiphenomena. They were common in John's day. They persist today.

John of the Cross is best known for his description of the *dark night of the senses* and the *dark night of the Spirit*. Note very carefully that they are *two* things. The dark night of the senses is the renunciation of all things one appreciates. The author of *The*

Cloud of Unknowing suggests something similar in the term "the cloud of forgetting." This not only includes material things, but relationships with family and friends, and spiritual consolations (e.g., visions, conversations with God, etc.). It is not just a matter of renouncing sin, but of cutting off everything that keeps the soul from flying as a bird to God, who is totally other. Such a person seeks the most difficult, repulsive, and uncomfortable style of life.

John believes that one comes to God through "dark faith."

> The soul, in order to be effectively guided to this state [of union with God] by faith, must not only be in darkness with respect to that part that concerns the creatures and the temporal things, which is the sensual and lower part, . . . but likewise that it must be blinded and darkened according to that part which has respect to God and to spiritual things, which is the rational and higher part.

Please note with great care that this statement and the narrative from which it is taken is saying without any doubt that we are justified by grace through faith and not by any works of our own. The student needs to bear in mind that much of what is commonly identified with the Protestant Reformation is a product of the sixteenth-century mind—Protestant or Catholic—within the sociocultural world of Western Europe.

Dark faith leads us to the second dark night, that of the Spirit. John was very cautious, as we should be, about extraordinary phenomena—visions, what are called "locutions" (conversations with God), stigmata, etc.—because he believes they are obstacles to union with God. The dark night of the Spirit, which is more painful than the dark night of the senses, is characterized by alienation and isolation, in which the participant is unable to pray and unable to do normal duties.

> Why is the Divine light . . . here called by the soul a dark night? To this the answer is that for two reasons this Divine wisdom is not only night and darkness for the soul, but is

likewise affliction and torment. The first is because of the height of Divine Wisdom, which transcends the talent of the soul, and in this way is darkness to it; the second, because of its vileness and impurity, in which respect it is painful and afflictive to it, and is also dark.

One needs to keep in mind images of the vision of God as the perception of darkness throughout the history of Christian spirituality, as in Gregory of Nyssa, Bonaventure, and the author of *The Cloud of Unknowing*. St. John of the Cross may appear rather grim. He conceived of the union with God, which was his abiding passion, as a spiritual marriage, just as did Teresa. This he describes, particularly in the *Spiritual Canticle,* which was a meditation upon the Song of Songs, with great beauty.

Instrumental Images
  Spiritual Exercises.
  Method in meditation.
    Composition of place.
    Use of the senses.
    Rhythm.
    Word-by-word reflection.
    Colloquy.
  Degrees of prayer.
    Discursive, recollective, quiet, union.
    The seven "rooms."
  Dark night of the senses.
  Dark night of the soul.
  Dark faith.
  Consolation and desolation.
  Betrothal.

Terminal Images
  To the greater glory of God.
  Spiritual marriage.
  Union of likeness.

SELECT BIBLIOGRAPHY

Ignatius Loyola, *The Spiritual Exercises,* translated by Louis J. Puhl. Loyola, 1951.

John of the Cross, *Ascent of Mt. Carmel,* translated by Allison Peers. Doubleday, 1959.

————, *Dark Night of the Soul,* translated by Allison Peers. Doubleday, 1959.

————, *Living Flame of Love,* translated by Allison Peers. Doubleday, 1971.

Teresa of Avila, *Autobiography,* translated by Allison Peers. Doubleday, 1972.

————, *Interior Castle,* translated by Allison Peers. Doubleday, 1972.

————, *Way of Perfection,* translated by Allison Peers. Doubleday, 1972.

The Italian School

While the Renaissance never really touched Spain, much less the Reformation, Italy was at the center of it, which influenced Italian spirituality both negatively—as a reaction against the "paganism" of the Renaissance—and positively. There is a grace or lightness to Italian spirituality of this period, in which the humanism of the Renaissance was a positive influence. There is also a practicality which is very different from the abstract, bare-bones austerity of the Spaniards. The austerity of the Italians is veiled. Perhaps Pourrat is correct in saying that the Reformation made no real impact in Italy because "its coldness, lacking all ascetic form, with nothing to appeal to the senses, bewildered the expansive Italian temperament, which yearns for outward demonstration."

The Italian school was not very theologically sophisticated. It was inclined to contemplate the inward disposition of Jesus. It embraced art, as we would hope, at a time when the greatest Italian artists flourished. Christianity, for the Italian school, was above all a religion of love. In a century which was obsessed with

the issue of divine providence, grace, free will, and predestination—there were Roman Catholic theologians who agreed with
Calvin—the Italian school tended to be Molinist, a theological
position taught by Luis de Molina, a Spanish jurist. He argued
for *virtual* predestination, as pertains to God's foreknowledge, as
opposed to *formal* predestination. Formal predestination teaches
that God does not give his grace to all, while virtual predestination insists that he does, knowing that not all will consent to it
and will therefore be damned by God, who knows this in advance. Virtual predestination, believe it or not, was considered
the liberal viewpoint.

Whereas there are distinguished members of the Italian
school—e.g., Jerome Savonarola (1452–1498), a Dominican and
a Thomist whose prophetic utterances angered the politicians of
his day and got him executed; Cajetan (1480–1547), who was the
founder of the Theatines and who is not to be confused with his
contemporary, Thomas de Vio Cajetan (1469–1534), the misin-
terpreter of Aquinas; and Robert Bellarmine (1542–1621), a Jesuit, a very reasonable man who once debated with James I (VI) of
England and supported Galileo—only one writer the unknown
author of the *Spiritual Combat,* is to be especially noted here. The
book in its original form was probably written by LAWRENCE
SCUPOLI (1530–1610), a Theatine. The *Spiritual Combat,* by its
very name bespeaks a dualism between the goodness of God and
the depravity of man, a motif inherited from the fifteenth century
and beloved of sixteenth- and seventeenth-century humanity
(with a lapse again in the nineteenth century). The summit of
perfection is achieved by fighting against self, by an inward mortification. There are four things that we are to do: distrust ourselves, trust God, use well the faculties of soul and body—i.e., understanding, will, and the senses—and, pray. We are to crush
the passions one by one, to keep watch over the body, and to
pray. It is out of this spirit that the excesses—self-flagellation,
hair shirts, deprivation of sleep, etc.—identified with moritifica-
tion arose.

The reader needs to keep in mind that *Spiritual Combat* could have been written by a Puritan in New England just as well as an Italian canon regular. The trappings are very different, but the essence of the *Weltanschauung* is much the same. *Spiritual Combat* was very popular in the Russian Orthodox spiritual renewal in the nineteenth century, perhaps most notably identified with Theophan the Recluse (1815–1894).

Instrumental Images
Fighting against self.
Inward and outward mortification.

Terminal Images
Inward disposition of Jesus.
Predestination.

SELECT BIBLIOGRAPHY
Lawrence Scupoli, *Spiritual Combat*. Paulist, 1978.

The French School

Hilda Graef writes, "Though the seventeenth century still produced some attractive mystics and a certain amount of mystical theology, it, and even more the eighteenth century of rationalism and 'enlightenment,' was a period of decline." It lacked originality and theological insight, she goes on to say. We will return to the sixteenth century briefly to pick up Protestant mysticism, but we need first to touch on the French and English schools.

The founder (in one sense) of the French school was FRANCIS DE SALES (1567–1622). A bishop, a director of souls, and a man of action, he sought to combine Ignatian and Carmelite (particularly that of Teresa) spirituality. The end result was fuzzy and subjective. He was also guided by the Italian spirit of air, flight, and space. Hoffman said of Francis, "He is representative of the feeling-for-life [*Lebensgefuhl*] of Catholic Baroque times, of a '*devout humanism*'." He was not overly concerned for the etiquette of piety, but in offering a way for souls to find union with God.

His most famous disciple was Jeanne de Chantal (1752–1641), a noble lady with whom he founded the Congregation of the Visitation (1610) for women who could not take the austere life of the Carmelites and the Poor Clares (the "second order" of St. Francis, considered the most rigorous order in the Roman Catholic Church, as well as the Anglican, founded by Clare [Feast day: August 11], follower of Francis of Assisi). Frances de Sales' *Introduction to the Devout Life,* his best known work, was written for laity and teaches a simple form of meditation known as the Salesian method. It is sometimes taught in the Episcopal Church as *the* way to meditate.

The Salesian meditation has five steps:

1. Preparation
   a) Place yourself in the presence of God.
   b) Pray for assistance.
   c) Compose the place (i.e., imagine a scene from the life of Jesus).
2. Considerations: identify those images in the scene that affect you.
3. Affections and Resolutions: convert feelings into understanding and then resolutions (acts of the will).
4. Conclusion
   a) Thanksgiving.
   b) Oblation or offering of the results of the meditation.
   c) Petition to fulfill in your life this day its insights.
5. The Spiritual Nosegay: that which we carry through the day from the meditation.

The "spiritual nosegay," which is a distinctive mark of Salesian meditation, is a clue to Francis de Sales' spirituality. A nosegay is a little bunch of sweet-smelling flowers which ladies and gentlemen of the period carried with them when they went outdoors, so they could travel without being overcome by the stench of the open sewers that commonly ran along the streets of European cities.

A curious teaching of Francis de Sales, which eventually leads to the heresy of quietism—the quest for complete passivity and annihilation of the will, taught by Miguel de Molinos (1628–1696) (by no means to be confused with Luis), and occasionally taught by the slippery FRANCIS FENELON (1651–1715)—is "holy indifference." We are to be like statues—Ignatius says corpses, which is too strong for Francis—and to stand in the corner where the maker puts us. If he wants us to go to hell, says Francis, that is fine! Once again we see in this the projection on God of the image of the absolute monarch which prevailed in Europe at this time. It is not a matter of whether such a God is "fair."

One should be careful, however, about too close a correlation between Francis de Sales and Miguel de Molinos. The former, for example, insisted upon the need for spiritual guides. The latter thought they were absurd.

There is in Francis' teaching the image of *liquefaction,* which is analogous to the oceanic feeling described by William James, Abraham Marlow, and others in this century. He describes that point at which the participant feels herself flowing into what she loves. The center of the experience moves out of the mind into an experience of love—like the prayer of the heart in Byzantine mysticism. Like John of the Cross, Francis speaks disparagingly of mystical phenomena—levitations, visions, raptures, etc.—because he thinks these things stand in the way. He is, unlike John of the Cross, optimistic and confident of the victory of God's love.

This optimistic spirit is not true in the piety that followed Francis in France. A growing pessimism characterizes English and French thought as it moves more deeply into the seventeenth century. For this reason Francis de Sales is considered an alien figure in the general tenor of the French school by many scholars. The very complex and paradoxical figures of Cardinal Richelieu (1585–1642)—of Dumas' *Three Musketeer* fame—and even more, PIERRE DE BERULLE (1575–1629), who is almost as seemingly contradictory, lie behind the continuing evolution of seventeenth-century French spirituality. In 1611 Berulle founded the French version of the Oratory of PHILIP NERI. Philip Neri was an Italian priest, particularly famous as a confessor. The Oratory, named simply for the room in which a group of priests met with Philip Neri for religious renewal, is a congregation of secular—as opposed to religious (i.e., those in a religious order such as the Benedictines, Franciscans, Cistercians, etc.)—priests living together without vows. The Oratory emphasizes the witness of prayer, preaching, and the sacraments. They loved beautiful liturgy, with magnificent music. We get the musical term *oratorio* from the Oratory.

Berulle's theological bias, which influenced the Oratory of France, was Pauline and Augustinian, with Jansenist affinities. Jansenism is named for Cornelius Jansen (1585–1638), and is a Roman Catholic theology strongly akin to Puritan thought. It holds to the total depravity of humanity and the irresistible nature of grace. For Berulle, therefore, grace is the central issue, and personal abnegation is very important. Nature is nothingness. He was very christocentric and, not surprisingly, begins with the servitude of Christ's humanity.

These themes, which one can readily see are contrary to the optimism of Francis de Sales, were enlarged by JEAN-JACQUES OLIER (1608–1657), who was a member of the Oratory and the founder of a school of priests at St. Sulpice, then a suburb of Paris. For Olier the Holy Spirit takes possession of us by annihilating us, reducing us to nothingness. But as one commentator says, "His Augustinian pessimism is moderated through a deep mysticism and a profound lyrical style." For Olier our only hope is adherence to the humanity of Christ, which requires eucharistic adoration, devotions to the Sacred Heart, and the rosary.

These three devotional practices are, of course, not original with seventeenth-century France. They go back to various points in time. Bernard mentions the Sacred Heart, Benediction began in the fourteenth century, and the Rosary seems to have evolved slowly among the Cistercians and the Dominicans from the twelfth and thirteenth centuries. With the exception of Benediction, they are not to be condemned—and while Benediction is bad theology, it has an aesthetic appeal like Italian opera. The Rosary is a device consonant with a universal principle of contemplation that at the center of ascetical theology has simplicity and repetition. But in seventeenth-century France the fascination with these became symptomatic of a growing sentimentality.

JOHN EUDES (1601–1680), a younger disciple of Berulle and sometime member of the Oratory, is the name usually associated with the excessive devotional practice of this time. For Eudes, the Feast of the Sacred Heart of Jesus sums up all other feasts. With Eudes, the church is reaching to a spiritual nadir only equaled by Nikolaus Zinzendorf's (1700–1760) "religion of the heart" and his Herrnhut cult of the Five Wounds, which developed in German Protestant pietism almost a century later.

The difference between Francis de Sales and the Oratory can be seen clearly when we contrast the method of meditation in the Oratory—called the Sulpician method—with the Salesian method. The process is similar, but not the focus.

1. Preparation
    a) Place oneself in the presence of God.
    b) Recognition of our unworthiness: think about our sins.
    c) Recognize our inability to help ourselves.
2. Body of meditation
    a) Adoration: consideration of the subject (a scene from the Life of Jesus).
    b) Communion: contrition, reflection upon our lukewarmness, and petition for grace.

3. Cooperation and resolution: movement from feeling through intellect to will.
4. Conclusion
   a) Prayer of thanksgiving.
   b) Prayer for pardon.
   c) Spiritual nosegay.

The priests of the Oratory and St. Sulpice were anti-Molinist—i.e., they held to formal predestination—but they were not true Jansenists. They are not to be confused, therefore, with the community at Port-Royal, a Cistercian convent which, from 1622 to its dissolution by the church in 1709, was a center for Jansenist thought. The Jansenists and the Jesuits were particular enemies. The Jansenists were theological determinists—i.e., we have no choice about whether we go to heaven or hell. We are predestined. They were also moral rigorists. The casuistry of the Jesuits was considered anathema. Today we would describe the Jesuits as Christian humanists, the Jansenists as evangelicals.

BLAISE PASCAL (1623–1662), a distinguished mathematician and philosopher, was influenced by Port-Royal and his sister was a nun there. His best known religious work, *Pensees* ("*Thoughts*"), is centered on Christ as Savior and Pascal's own personal experience of salvation. This is consistent with the well-known quotation from Pascal, "The heart has reasons of which reason knows not." This same notion, interestingly enough, was condemned by Innocent XI along with sixty-seven other ideas of Miguel Molinos, the founder of quietism. Of Molinos it is said, "Indifference was the center of his inward life." That ought to be called in question, but he also said, as Pascal did, "He who loves God in the way reason argues or the intellect understands, does not love the true God." John Henry Newman argued the same thing two centuries later and it was considered by many the greatest Roman Catholic theology of nineteenth-century England.

Pascal was not, strictly speaking, of the French school. He is included here because he is a distinguished representative from the Roman Catholic tradition of a theological position—be it Jansenist or Puritan (in the sense of the Synod of Dort, 1618–1619)—that develops into a religion of the heart, devotion to Jesus (Jesusolatry), personal and individual experience of salvation, etc., which becomes common in American piety. Quietism and pietism were very much alike. Both reflected a simplistic interpretation of Jansenist or Puritan theology, and both made a profound impression on English and American evangelicalism, as we shall see. Much of both became what is known as fideism, which is a subjective and anti-intellectual appeal to the authority of individual experience, devoid of reason. Fideism was condemned at the First Vatican Council (1869–1870).

Instrumental Images
   Devout humanism or Baroque sensibility.
   Salesian meditation (particularly a "spiritual nosegay").
   Holy indifference (leading to quietism).
   Abnegation and irresistable grace.
   Eucharistic Devotion (Benediction), Sacred Heart, and Rosary.
   Sulpician meditation (emphasis upon unworthiness).
   The reasons of the heart.

Terminal Images
   Liquefaction.
   Predestination.

SELECT BIBLIOGRAPHY
Francis Fenelon, *Christian Perfection,* translated by Mildred W. Stillman. Bethany Press, 1976.
Blaise Pascal, *Pensees,* translated by W. L. Trotter. Dutton, 1958.
Francis de Sales, *Introduction to the Devout Life,* translated by John K. Ryan. Harper, 1950.
———, *Treatise on the Love of God,* translated by Henry B. Mackey. Greenwood, 1942.

The English School

A distinguished Roman Catholic is included in the English school and then we move on to the Caroline divines, who had particular impact upon the evolution of Christian spirituality.

DOM AUGUSTINE BAKER (1575–1641) was a Roman Catholic priest in England when that was not a safe thing to be. Baker's teaching is found in a collection of his writings entitled *Holy Wisdom*. He is in the tradition of the fourteenth-century English mystics, particularly the author of *The Cloud of Unknowing* and Walter Hilton. He was an English individualist with the temperament of a refined recluse. He advocated a detachment of the person from all things, including liturgy and private devotion or meditation "in the proper manner."

One can easily appreciate the aversion of Baker to the tyranny of spiritual directors, imposing their "system" on unsuspecting novices. He was a healthy antidote to spiritual scrupulosity. At the same time, as Thomas Merton points out, Baker's disinterest in liturgy and meditation in favor of contemplative introversion—"navel gazing," some would say—initiated in Western thought, particularly English and American, the erroneous notion that there is a great gulf fixed between action and contemplation, the world of the mystic and the world of the student of Scripture and participant in the sacraments. People confuse the contemplative life with quietism and even Pelagianism.

Immediate post-Reformation Anglican piety has implicit, but few explicit, roots in fourteenth-century English spirituality. Its clearly expressed ground is the Book of Common Prayer, which is not only the symbol, but is the actuality of Anglican unity in the midst of a world where Roman Catholic and Puritan theologies and pieties are pressing on either side. Anglicanism did not have the benefit of a clear, theological rationale at a time when such clarity was highly prized and where intuitive devotion was not readily endorsed. But it retains a deep commitment to the liturgy and the sacraments.

RICHARD HOOKER (c. 1554–1600; Feast day: November 3) was

the initial apologist for the Elizabethan settlement of 1559. His *Treatise on the Laws of Ecclesiastical Polity* is a defense of episcopacy, not a discussion of ascetical theology; but it established some guideposts for those in the seventeenth century who did write more specifically on spirituality. Hooker was a Christian humanist. He drew on the Church Fathers and was obviously indebted to Thomas Aquinas. He avoided the rationalism of the Puritans and the subjectivism of the Lutherans and the pessimism of both. There is a kind of chastened optimism about him. All of this and more formed a theological basis for what was to follow. We need to keep in mind, however, that Hooker was a moralist, not a metaphysician (as Aquinas), and therefore, English theology as influenced by Hooker, including ascetical theology, always has a moral intention. It wants to influence how we live in this world with other people.

It is clear also that the *Imitation of Christ,* the classic of the *Devotio moderna,* and the *Introduction to the Devout Life* were widely read in seventeenth-century England. One might wish for something a little less sentimental, because, when combined with a natural Anglican pastoral versus methodological bias, the end result was and is what someone has called "sloppy agapè" (i.e., excessive sentimentality). The fuzziness of Anglican ascetical theology is clear in the persistent advocacy of meditation, but its confusion then and now is with Bible study. They are not the same thing, but the difference becomes clear only when one examines the two distinct methods.

It is extremely important to note two characteristics about Anglican spirituality in this period. First, it is rooted in the liturgy. Contrary to the spirit of Bernard and Francis, it comes right out of the Daily Office. This is related to the Benedictine spirit which has always influenced English spirituality. The second thing to note is that it celebrates the Creation. Mainstream Anglicanism is unalterably opposed to the dualism of the Jansenists and Puritans and is in accord with the insights of the Victorines (Hugh and Richard et al.), Francis de Sales, Walter Hilton, Julian of Norwich, etc. There are those even today who consider Anglicans weak on sin and the doctrine of the Atonement. Whereas there is always the possibility that this ongoing viewpoint is in error, it is not a new or theologically barren position.

In the previous section it is suggested that there is a relationship between the French Baroque and French piety in the seventeenth century. This reinforces a concern in this study for the identification of the sociology of prayer. It is also argued on occasion that there is no Baroque in seventeenth-century England. JOHN DONNE (c. 1573–1631; Feast day: March 31), the first of the so-called five Caroline "metaphysical poets" (Herbert, Vaughan, Traherne, and Crashaw are the others), is possibly a refutation of that claim. He is exemplary of the "age mannerism," a period given to a precious rhetorical style. "Mannerism" has a kind of restraint. It is a search after an image that will evoke a presence. But the image is very fragile. Obviously this is a highly speculative, rational approach to God, but it is also strongly affective.

Donne wrote magnificent and sensual love poetry. He was a Christian humanist. He was an exponent of the "witty" sermon, which played upon every possible nuance of a text to make its point, drawing heavily upon classical sources. He was a man of great intellectual power. Yet he was clearly influenced by Ignatian discipline and, as Louis Bouyer says, he was able to "reaccomodate all the emotional side of medieval piety within Anglicanism." This is not surprising, since he came from a Roman Catholic family. Martin Thornton claims Donne is "a sister" to Margery Kempe. Donne, unlike Kempe, can sometimes be a bit of a schoolmaster, didactic and compulsive. He was a person of discipline, whose passion could only be satisfied in faith as an act of will.

Donne, like other Caroline spiritual masters, was fascinated by death—perhaps an inheritance from the fifteenth century. When one reads his poetry—the revival of interest in which we owe to T. S. Eliot—the rich imagery often leaves one with a slight sense

of gloom. Yet Donne insists that "all divinity is love, or wonder." His piety is speculative and kataphatic. He retains a Baroque delight in contradiction and tension. Everything is ashes,
including our most intense love of one another, unless it resolves
itself in the life in God. It is not surprising that the "holy son-
nets" of Donne, with their bittersweet quality, reflect the death
of his wife, Ann Moore (1618). His obsession with death, however, needs to be balanced with his erotic poetry.

Donne was not one who wanted to leave this world. He was
fascinated, however, with the relation of the body to the soul,
and in the style of his age, he played with the question. For example, *Extasie,* which begins as an amorous love poem resolves
into a discussion of the relationship of body and soul.

> But O alas, so long, so farre
>   Our bodies why doe we forbeare?
> They are ours, though they are not wee, Wee are
>   The intelligences, they are the spheares.

There is an implicit Neo-Platonic allusion here, even if it is a bit
muddled. (The spheres themselves are not the bodies.) This is
quite in accord with the "amorous Neo-Platonism" characteristic
of the Renaissance. In other words, the eros of the irrational soul
becomes more "fleshed out" and of interest to a John Donne than
to a Gregory of Nyssa.

There is a kind of ladder in Donne's thinking, which has been
identified by at least one scholar. It begins with conversion,
moves to contrition, is followed by cleansing, and is consummated in joy. This is as systematic as an English divine of this
period could be expected to be.

Many of us, when we think of Donne, recall almost immedi-
ately the words, "No man is an Island, intire of itselfe; . . . any
man's death diminishes me, because I am involved in Mankinde;
And therefore never send to know for whom the bell tolls; it tolls
for thee." Equally moving are Donne's words from this familiar
sonnet.

> Death be not proud, though some have called thee
> Mighty and dreadful, for, thou art not soe,
> For, those, who thou think'st, thou dost overthrow,
> Die not, poore death, nor yet canst thou kill mee.
>
> . . . .
> One short sleepe past, wee wake eternally,
> And death shall be no more; death, thou shalt die.

More fun is Donne's apparent play, in the witty mannerism of his times, upon the name of his wife, Ann Moore, and himself in *A Hymne to God the Father*. This poem, perhaps in the light of "amorous Neo-Platonism," poses more directly the relationship of human sexuality to the spiritual ascent, and may indeed mark the growth of an awareness that the eros of the irrational soul of Neo-Platonism, which motivates the soul's ascent, is indeed rooted in our sexuality.

> Wilt thou forgive the sinne where I begunne,
>   Which is my sinne, though it were done before?
> Wilt thou forgive those sinnes, through which I runne,
>   And do run still: though I do still deplore?
> When thou has done, thou hast not done,
>   For, I have more.
>
> Wilt thou forgive that sinne by which I'have wonne
>   Others to sinne? and, made my sinne their doore?
> Wilt thou forgive that sinne which I shunne
>   A yeare, or two: but wallowed in, a score?
> When thou hast done, thou hast not done,
>   For I have more.
>
> I have a sinne of feare, that when I have spunne
>   My last thred, I shall perish on the shore;
> Sweare by thy selfe, that at my death thy sonne
>   Shall shine as he shines now, and theretofore;
>   And have done that, Thou haste donne,
>   I feare no more.

LANCELOT ANDREWES (1555–1626; Feast day: September 26), is called by Bouyer the "spiritual master" of Anglicanism. He was a pastor, a man of great erudition, and a mystic. He was one of the translators of the Authorized Version of the Bible. Like most Caroline divines, he believed strongly in the value of catechism and spiritual guidance, as well as the sermon, as means of developing a personal ascetical practice. He was a distinguished preacher. The Eucharist was central for his piety. Therefore, he was opposed to Calvinism, refusing to be in the Anglican delegation to the Synod of Dort (1618).

Andrewes principal spiritual work was a collection of his private prayers, *Preces privatae*. Written originally in Latin, they reveal a strong influence of Greek Christianity, which was characteristic of some of seventeenth-century Anglicanism. "No book of prayers could be more obviously English, yet more varied in its sources," writes Martin Thornton.

Mention must be made of JEREMY TAYLOR (1613–1667; Feast day: August 13). He was a chaplain in the Royalist army during the English Civil War, which says much about his commitments. FitzSimons Allison, Church historian and parish priest, claims that English piety has gone astray ever since Taylor, whom he accuses of being Pelagian. It is probably more accurate to say that he is typical of English spirituality. According to Bouyer, "He was characteristic of an average, if not a mediocre, Anglicanism in which a deeply poetic culture gave fulness to the commonplaces which otherwise would have bordered on platitude." Another phrase descriptive of Taylor, quoted in several places, is that his writings "are characteristic expressions of Anglican spirituality in their balanced sobriety and their insistence on a well-ordered piety which stresses temperance and moderation in all things."

Taylor was a casuist, a teacher of moral theology. He embodies that Caroline unity of moral and ascetical theology. His *Ductor dubitatium (Teacher of Doubtful Cases)* is a heavy, moral exposition of that chastened optimism characteristic of Anglicanism, of which mention has already been made. It is ironic that in the Preface to this ponderous volume Taylor writes, "What God has made plain, men have intricated." Would that we understood this "plainness," rather than having to labor through Taylor's pedantic work.

Taylor's ascetical works, *Rules and Exercises in Holy Living* (1650) and *Rules and Exercises in Holy Dying* (1651) were written because he believed that under the Puritans there was no good teaching. *Holy Living* is a dull exposition of the growth toward perfection, advocating habitual recollection upon the world, and frequent, short prayer. Dull as it undoubtedly is, this expresses the English concern with the question of how one lives the ordinary, routine Christian life (which is what is meant by "habitual recollection"). *Holy Dying* is a splendidly macabre book, which teaches us little, but is inspiring for its faith. The danger is that, like other Anglican spiritual writings, it can be seen as merely quaint.

One thing of a more innovative nature for which Taylor is remembered is his suggestion that marriage exists for friendship, as well as procreation. This novel notion, with a faint recollection of another Englishman who wrote on friendship in the monastery as the way to Christ—Aelred of Rievaulx—suggests a yet undeveloped theme of spirituality: marriage as the path to Christ.

The convoluted thoughts of Donne, the erudition of Andrews, and the pedantry of Taylor—all of which can obscure the deep spirituality of each—are perhaps transcended by the second and only other of the metaphysical poets of whom I would make specific mention here, GEORGE HERBERT (1593–1633; Feast day: February 27). Herbert thought of himself as a country parson, but he was also a man of considerable rhetorical skill. He has been called a "populist metaphyscian." Through reflection in prayer, the daily Office, and the Eucharist, he wrote his poems to give meaning to his life and the ordinary lives of those people to whom he was called to minister. He cared for people. There is no cold detachment in him, as in John of the Cross or Jean-Jacques Olier. "Julian is spiritual mother to George Herbert," says

Thornton. Optimistic, warm, he is the embodiment of the English pastoral spirituality at its best. As all those we have mentioned, he is kataphatic and affective.

In an introduction to Herbert's work Anne Fremantle and W. H. Auden say, "Herbert assumes the Christian sensibility of his audience, and the dialogue with Christ which is the substance of his finest poems is among the most personal and affecting in the English mystical tradition." It was T. S. Eliot who said that sensibility—the ability to express a comprehensive, balanced whole in experience—reaches an end in English literature with the metaphysical poets, including Herbert.

Herbert's poems were collected in a work which he himself called *The Temple: Sacred Poems and Private Ejaculations.* He described these meditations—for that they are—from his deathbed as "a picture of the many spiritual conflicts that have passed between God and my soul, before I could subject mine to the will of Jesus my Master, in whose service I have now found perfect freedom." They embody a constant conflict within Herbert, not as some thought between the secular world and the vocation of the priest, but, far more subtly, they bespeak the conflict with self-will. Herbert knew the struggle of the spiritual life. Simone Weil, a major spiritual figure of our own century, wrote that reading one of Herbert's poems was a turning point for her in her own struggle, Ralph Vaughan-Williams, the great English composer, set it and four others of Herbert's works to music, entitling them "Five Mystical Songs." This particular poem reads:

Love bad me welcome: yet my soul drew back,
    Guiltie of dust and sinne.
But quick-ey'd Love, observing me grow slack
    From my first entrance in,
Drew nearer to me, sweetly questioning,
    If I lack'd anything.

A guest, I answer'd, worthy to be here:
    Love said, You shall be he.

> I the unkinde, ungratefull? Ah my deare,
>> I cannot look on thee.
> Love took my hand, and smiling did reply,
>> Who made the eyes but I?
>
> Truth Lord, but I have marr'd them, let my shame
>> Go where it doth deserve.
> And know you not, sayes Love, who bore the blame?
>> My deare, then I will serve.
> You must sit down, sayes Love, and taste my meat;
>> So I did sit and eat.

It has been suggested that the poems of Herbert have a cat-
echetical intention which, combined with the work of his friend,
Nicholas Ferrar, sought to bring a spiritual theology to the English church. He was a well-read theologian and a remarkable
poet, thoroughly in control of his craft. This poem on the Trinity
is a clear illustration of the power and subtlety of Herbert, who
understood the age of mannerism and, at the same time, transcended it to convey in delicate, constrained images, eternal
truth.

> Lord, who has form'd me out of mud,
>> And hast redeem'd me through thy bloud,
>> And sanctifi'd me to do good;
>
> Purge all my sinnes done heretofore:
>> For I confess my heavie score,
>> And I will strive to sinne no more.
>
> Enrich my heart, mouth, hands in me,
>> With faith, with hope, with charitie;
> That I may runne, rise, rest with thee.

Notice the play here with the number three.

Herbert is a superb embodiment of the Anglican spirit. He
strives for reason, balance, contrition; but he will have nothing to

do with despair and fills his poetry with a kind of radiant, diffused light.

Izaak Walton, about whom it must suffice to comment that aside from an extraordinarily long life (he died at ninety!) he was the prototypical Anglican lay ecclesiastical dilletante, tells in his life of George Herbert that the latter sent a copy of *The Temple* from his deathbed to NICHOLAS FERRAR (1592–1637; Feast day: December 1), his close friend and perhaps the purest expression of Anglican lay piety—although Ferrar was in deacon's orders—of that century and maybe any other. Ferrar is not to be remembered for his writings. They were largely destroyed when the Roundheads burned his house in 1646. He considered the pope the anti-Christ and the Puritans considered him a papist. Yet in his semi-monastic retreat at Little Gidding he developed a magnificent experiment, rooted in the Bible and the Book of Common Prayer. Martin Thornton suggests it is Benedictine in spirit, as England has always been. Here was a living example of austere Anglican asceticism.

T. S. Eliot commemorated the spirit of Little Gidding and Nicholas Ferrar in the last of his *Four Quartets,* which closes with these words,

With the drawing of this Love and the voice of this Calling

We shall not cease from exploration
And the end of all our exploring
Will be to arrive where we started
And know the place for the first time. . . .

Quick now, here, now always—
A condition of complete simplicity
(Costing not less than everything)
And all shall be well and
All manner of thing shall be well
When the tongues of flame are in-folded
Into the crowned knot of fire
And the fire and the rose are one.

Within these lines there lies, of course, a quotation from Julian of Norwich as well.

After the Interregnum and the rest of the seventeenth century English spirituality goes downhill. In fact, WILLIAM LAW (1686–1761; Feast day: April 9), to mention one last name in this section, is the most noteworthy figure in English spirituality in this period. He was a nonjuror, which meant that he was an Anglican who could not look for preferment in the establishment because he believed the Stuarts, overthrown in 1688, to be the rightful kings of England and would not swear—which is what "nonjuror" means—allegiance to the Hanoverian kings. Of Law, Thornton says, "he was a transitional figure, looking back to the Caroline age and forward to the disintegration." His most notable work is *A Serious Call to a Devout and Holy Life,* which shows an influence from Tauler, Ruysbroeck, and Thomas à Kempis. Its very title implies a recollection of Bernard's *devotio,* which Law defines as follows: "Devotion signifies a life given or devoted to God. . . . The devout man . . . served God in everything."

Thornton describes the work, which has the curious eighteenth-century pedantic style, as more muddled than wrong. It is a curious combination of things, but has probably had more influence, after John Bunyan's *Pilgrim's Progress* and Francis de Sales' *Introduction to the Devout Life,* than any other post-Reformation spiritual writing. It made a definite impression on John Wesley and George Whitefield.

Thornton's dislike of Law's writings is tempered by the claim of John Booty, an Episcopal church historian, that Law "represented the heart of English spirituality during the sixteenth and seventeenth centuries." While Booty's statement is an exaggeration—Law was too much given to the division between private devotion and liturgical prayer, which modern piety inherited from the *Devotio moderna*—it is worthy of note. Booty believes that *The Spirit of Love,* a work composed after Law became interested in Jacob Boehme (see below) is Law's best effort.

Law's emphasis upon a disciplined prayer life and his witness to the depths and heights of the spiritual way is significant. Thankfully, he rejects bibliolatry. We can only rejoice in his denial of legalistic or forensic notions of the atonement, which have troubled Western theological thought since Anselm, as well as notions of humanity's total depravity. There is in humanity "a seed of life," "a smothered spark of heaven." One is reminded of the *scintilla animae,* the spark of God's love that ignites the soul. As Law wrote,

> For as love is the God that created all things, so love is the purity, the perfection, and blessing of all created things; and nothing can live in God but as it lives in love.

And then again he writes, "Now nothing wills and works with God but the spirit of love, because nothing else works in God himself." The reader is reminded of the mysticism of the Trinity found in Julian of Norwich, in William of St. Thierry, and ultimately in Augustine's *On the Trinity.*

As I have implied, Law had no appreciation for the spirituality of the Book of Common Prayer. He has no sense of corporate worship. He does combine, in the manner of the Caroline divines, moral and ascetic theology. But he is antirational after the manner of the fourteenth-century German Dominicans he admires, which perhaps explains his later fascination with Boehme. Bouyer observes that Law turns Boehme's "bizarre genius . . . into a very British kind of mild dottiness" in his later works. Yet Aldous Huxley considered Law the most saintly figure in all Anglicanism. Law came to hold that concern for politics and social issues subverts the religious life. He adds his voice to that of Dom Augustine Baker 150 years before, creating a false and dangerous dichotomy between the active and the contemplative life.

One concluding observation might be made about English spirituality, along with its French cousin. Both of them are heavy on asceticism, but there seem to be few genuine mystics in the lot. It says something about the seventeenth century and its particular bias.

Instrumental Images
    Meditation as Bible study.
    Book of Common Prayer (particularly the daily offices).
    Pastoral concerns.
    Sermon.
    Catechism.

Terminal Images
    God as creator.
    A holy death.

SELECT BIBLIOGRAPHY
Lancelot Andrewes, *Private Devotions*. Macmillan, 1961.
Augustine Baker, *Holy Wisdom*. Christian Classics, 1973.
John Donne, *Selected Poems*. Penguin, 1950.
George Herbert, *Poems*. Oxford, 1961.
Richard Hooker, *Of the Laws of Ecclesiastical Polity*. Harvard, 1979.
William Law, *A Serious Call to a Devout and Holy Life and The Spirit of Love,* edited by Paul G. Stanwood. Paulist, 1978.
Jeremy Taylor, *A Selection of His Works*. Folcroft, 1974.

Classical Protestantism

There is a tendency to think of the Protestant Reformation as a totally new thing and to assume a radical discontinuity between the church of the fifteenth century and the reformers of the sixteenth century. A more balanced view would avoid such an exaggerated position. Luther, Calvin, Zwingli, and others were very much the products of their age and in important ways differed from one another. There is a common viewpoint among antagonists—e.g., Calvin and Ignatius Loyola—underlying the po-

lemic, which viewpoint may not be shared by fellow reformers—
e.g., Calvin and Luther. We must be on our guard against too
easy a stereotyping of persons and their interpretation of Christian
spirituality, and realize that sixteenth century Western culture
provided a context out of which both the Reformation and
Counter Reformation emerged in continuity with the Christian
past.

MARTIN LUTHER (1483–1546) can be considered the last great
medieval man. He was less a product of rational humanism, as
Calvin was, and was more a son of the German monastic tradition. He read Eckhart and especially Tauler. He published twice
(1516 and 1518) a truncated manuscript of an anonymous late
fourteenth-century mystical treatise varyingly called *Theologica
Germanica, Theologia Deutsch,* or *German Theology.* The work is in
the same apophatic tradition, stemming from Dionysius, as Eckhart and Tauler. Luther said of the *Theologica Germanica* that, except for the Bible and Augustine, no book had ever taught him
more about God and Christ and the human condition. Luther is
very much in the German mystical tradition of *Wesonmystik* or the
mysticism of essence, which is rooted in Dionysian spirituality.

The whole concept of the individual's experience of salvation
by grace through faith is in the mystical tradition of the German
Dominicans. As Bengt Hoffman says in *Luther and the Mystics,*
"the consonance between Luther and his mystical soul-mates lies
in the *experience* of justification, not primarily in *cognition* about an
old biblical truth revisited" (Emphasis author's). The tradition
which expresses this experience has a tendency to quietism, growing out of a very pessimistic notion of humanity and a sense of an
infinite abyss between God and man. The remedy, by which we
can accept God's *imputed righteousness,* is a faith which is an *inward*
discovery. Luther's biblical studies made this belief explicit in a
manner which was not in Tauler and others; but the subjectivism
of Luther is fundamentally mystical, enabling a "full view and
clear apprehension [of God] in Christ," according to Rufus Jones.

As Luther's thought develops he seems to become more

antimystical. A number of Luther scholars, particularly those who think mysticism is unmanly, applaud this apparent change. Luther's teaching, first formed in the school of Eckhart, Tauler, and the *Theologica Germanica,* now becomes dogmatized, or institutionalized (this is to be descriptive, not judgmental) and detached from its intuitive source. The Scriptures become a prooftext, as if the insight was one conferred totally from the outside, rather than from a spiritual apprehension of the texts, in the light of Luther's individual struggle, and in terms of the sixteenth-century cultural bias.

Much is made by those who believe Luther opposed Christian spirituality of his attack upon the *Schwärmer,* a German word meaning "enthusiasts," "dreamers," or even "serpents." The *Schwärmer* were antinomian, docetic, pneumatic Christians, believing that God had called them out of the world into a new order of the Holy Spirit. This kind of enthusiasm is present at most times and certainly is expressive of the heretical, if not lunatic, fringe of mysticism. To equate Luther's condemnation of the *Schwärmer* with opposition to fourteenth-century mysticism would be the same as saying that someone today who opposed the neo-Pentecostals was against Simone Weil or Thomas Merton. As Hoffman points out, the Schwärmer are not typical of mysticism. He goes on to cite Heiko Oberman, who argues that Luther's attitude "did not change when he encounters Tauler's writings and the anonymous *Theologica Germanica.* Nor did it change fundamentally in the struggle against the *Schwärmer.*"

Luther's teaching was both forensic and personal. God in Christ does account us as righteous. We are not righteous, according to Luther, by virtue of what we do. But Christ is present to us now. Luther uses very vivid images to speak of our being joined now to Christ, and this does in fact necessitate a way of attending to that presence (ascetical theology) and an accounting of the signs that we are in that presence (mystical theology). His use of the term "trustlike faith" is, according to Hoffman, the same as the medieval "synderesis."

As Luther continued he sowed the seeds for a deep spirituality in spite of what some see as a dicontinuity between the "young" and the "mature" Luther. His translation of the Bible into German and the revision of the liturgy provided a rich source for a deep piety among the people, unknown for centuries despite the best intentions of the medieval church. No doubt the printing press made this possible. His teaching concerning the priesthood of all believers opened up a theological basis for a genuine lay spirituality unknown since patristic times.

JOHN CALVIN (1509–1564) was the first modern man in the sense that Luther was the last medieval man. He was trained as a lawyer and he was an intellectual. In many ways he was dry as dust. In place of Luther's subjectivism, with its mystical awareness that in spite of ourselves we are justified, Calvin taught that we are predestined before birth to heaven or hell. The issue is to know to which we are predestined. Since God is inscrutable, apparently more interested in himself than us, the problem becomes intense. Yet out of this theology of the totally "other," strangely enough, there grew a Puritan ascetism, which we have already seen in its Roman Catholic version in France and in its influence upon English spirituality. For Calvin taught a kind of discipline which led to a *fruito divina,* an anticipation of eternal beatitude, assuring one that one is elect. This is not a mystical image in the classical sense, because the *fruito divina* is more the enjoyment of this world's goods—a "Judaistic literalism." The *fruito divina* lies at the heart of Max Weber's thesis about Protestant asceticism and a capitalist economy, which was developed by Tawney in *Religion and the Rise of Capitalism.* Yet the notion ultimately produces a mysticism of consolation found in later Calvinism.

Calvin was a rationalist who rejected pilgrimages, fasting, almsgiving, and other ascetical practices. His notion of love is cerebral, not affective. The direct heirs of Calvin were the English Puritans, who despised Herbert's lovely poetry and burned Little Gidding to the ground because of its "abominable practices." Calvin lacked any appreciation for receptive consciousness or what is sometimes called "thinking with the left hand." But he was not without a spirituality. What Tauler and the *Theologica Germanica* were for Luther, the *Devotio moderna* and Gerson were for Calvin. The problem with Calvin is that like many great theologians he is contradictory—something which his disciples failed to understand. Despite his belief in justification as "once and for all," growth in Christ is very important for Calvin, even though the subjects destined to grow have already been decided by God. Growth or sanctification is the result of the action of the Holy Spirit. God orders the life of the saved, and Christ is the pattern of that ordered life. As in the fifteenth-century *Devotio moderna*, since God is a transcendent father, we basically look to Christ the son to imitate. Calvin is stronger; we are to be incorporated in Christ. Calvin likes the image of spiritual marriage for the union between Christ and the event. However, he takes his inheritance from the *Devotio moderna* one giant step further, reading it through his theology of imputed justification as well as sanctification. In so doing he, like Gerson, moves away from the sentimentality and weak soteriology of the *Devotio moderna*.

The concept which Lucien Joseph Richard, in *The Spirituality of John Calvin,* says dominates the spirituality of Calvin is first found in Gerson's *pietas*. Piety is the characteristic of the person, according to Calvin, who lives within the order of God. It is the attitude one has to a sixteenth-century father. Piety is grounded in a sense of dependence and reveals itself in service and worship. The pious person is obedient to God's law and loves his fellows. He is dutiful in meditation and prayer. Piety is a concept that would appeal to an intellectual such as Calvin. It is to be greatly regretted that his later followers miss its meaning.

What followed the genius of Luther and Calvin is not all that distinguished, save for a few notable exceptions. The first exception is JACOB BOEHME (1525–1624), a Lutheran, a student of alchemy, a visionary, a shoemaker in Görlitz, and a genius as well. How one so "unlearned," who never went more than a day's journey from home, knew the Jewish *Kabbalah*, the Neo-Platonism of the Renaissance, and the Hermetic medicine of Paracelsus appears at first beyond comprehension. Actually there were followers of these various schools of thought in Görlitz at that time, and what Boehme did was use them all—as well as his biblical learning—to explain his experiences of God.

Divine wisdom is central to Boehme. Bouyer speaks of his "theosophy," a teaching about the world based on mystical insight. There are a number of cardinal principles in his teaching. God is the ground of being or *Ungrund*—a concept that may come from the fourteenth-century Dominican mystics. J. A. T. Robinson made the same image popular in the 1960s in his book *Honest to God*. He got the notion from Paul Tillich, who was very fond of Boehme's thought. The visible world in Boehme is the "counter-stroke" of the spiritual world. He takes the material world very seriously. But good and evil are a cosmic reality. "Heaven and hell are present everywhere," Boehme says. "God is all. He is darkness and light." The divine life is communicated to humanity in an immediate way. "Christ lives essentially in the faith of those who have given themselves completely to him. . . . Human life is a counter-stroke of the divine will, in and with which God wills."

The very difficult vocabulary Boehme uses, his convoluted thought, and his sense of the immanence of God can make him appear to be extremely odd. Thornton says he taught "exotic heresies." Many have concurred in that judgment, including at one time Boehme's own pastor. I am not so sure. There is no question of his genuine commitment to Christ. His understanding of the mystical experience as "the experience of God" is in accord both with Bernard and Luther's concept of faith. There is no doubt he goes beyond Luther, but he is still in his tradition.

Many of Boehme's images are from classical Christian mysticism. For example, he tells us that we go to God in prayer "with naked breath and words." The author of *The Cloud of Unknowing* says the same thing. He tells us that the experience of God is one of fire and light. As we have seen, this is common to transcendental experience and finds a home in John Wesley's Aldersgate experience, where he finds his "heart strangely warmed." Boehme speaks of the "sweetness of God," which is an image that weaves itself through Christian masters, including Calvin, in all ages. I suspect C. S. Lewis is referring to the same thing when he uses the German word, *Sehnsucht,* which means a "longing, pining, or yearning for God." It is not unrelated to Gregory of Nyssa's understanding of eros.

There is a strong affinity to C. G. Jung's thought in Boehme, which may be because of their use of similar sources. Jung is sometimes considered "exotic." The coincidence of opposites is very prominent in Boehme, which was beloved by both Jung and the nineteenth-century Romantics. Certainly Boehme influenced Hegel and German idealism, which in turn conjures up the fear of romanticism in some people. Boehme is not anti-intellectual, however, which romanticism at its worst is.

Perhaps Bouyer is right in saying that, while we can find Boehme stimulating and sometimes insightful, we have to move beyond his system to find ultimate direction in the spiritual life. As a theosophy it is more mystical than ascetical. He offers no method, but a vision strangely framed in a vocabulary that is usually foreign, sometimes fascinating, and uniquely his own. Boehme's admirers frequently say he must be read repeatedly, with a kind of intuitive receptivity, to be truly appreciated. He is not for action-mode, structured English minds, like Thornton.

Perhaps as surprising in their way are two Puritans who call into question the usual stereotype of the dour, ascetical Calvinist. The first is FRANCIS ROUS (1579–1669). Rous was Speaker of the House of Parliament under the Commonwealth and, as we can imagine, an ardent Puritan. Yet he believed that there is "something divine," like unto a *logos spermatikos* or *scintilla animae,* which is the eye of the soul (as opposed to the eye of reason). It helps to recall that Richard Rolle and Julian of Norwich spoke of an "inner" or "spiritual" eye. When this "something divine" is touched by the Scripture it is united to God. Rous, like Calvin himself, seems to be influenced by fourteenth-century bridal mysticism, because his favorite mystical image is the spiritual marriage. As many Christian spiritual masters, Rous wrote a commentary on the Song of Songs. Rous is one of those commentators for whom, unlike Origen, the individual and not the Church is the bride.

Rous also bears a resemblance to John of the Cross. The spiritual marriage is not achieved in this world, but only the betrothal—but Puritans took betrothals very seriously. We exist here in tribulation, but that is our glory. As Rous writes, "When the wine of natural joy is spent and there is nothing left but the water of affliction, than doth Christ turn this water into wine." This insight, which we have heard before and we hear again, is put in such a way that it is worth carrying as a "spiritual nosegay."

Then there is the remarkable THOMAS GOODWIN (1600–1680), chaplain to Oliver Cromwell. He is the Protestant John Eudes. The prevailing image for him is the heart of Christ. The point is for Christ's heart to dwell in our hearts. The Holy Spirit is first and foremost in the heart of Christ, and the Spirit seeks to subsume our hearts to Christ's heart. As Bouyer explains, "Just as Christ has his divine fullness in his personal union with the Godhead, he wants for himself a human fullness in his union consummated with all mankind." Here we have a Puritan devotion to the Sacred Heart.

RICHARD BAXTER (1615–1691) is an English Puritan who is not as surprising as Rous and Goodwin but is equally interesting in his own way. He wrote a treatise to counter George Herbert's *Country Parson,* entitled *Reformed Pastor.* He was a chaplain in Cromwell's army. But more important, he was as obsessed as any Calvinist with the question: How do I know I have saving faith? His answer in *The Saints' Everlasting Rest* is, in the final analysis, that we know this if we meditate regularly. He admits that the method he advises goes back to the fifteenth century and lies behind Garcia Ximenes de Cisneros and Ignatius Loyola. He is more rigid than Ignatius ever was, however.

We must not be too hard on Baxter. He wanted to make things simple, which usually gets us in trouble because we end up being moralistic and pietistic. Boehme was making quite an impact on England and he was very much against the "sect of the Boehmenists." He also wanted his theology clear, unlike Harry Vane, one time governor of the Massachusetts Bay Colony and architect of Cromwell's Commonwealth, whom he accused of being very obscure. (It is helpful to keep in mind the developing American colonies and the relation of English Puritan spirituality to New England and Caroline spirituality to Virginia. Nicholas Ferrar, for example, participated in the Virginia Company.)

Baxter's poetry has a straightforward, endearing quality to it, which speaks as well for him as anything.

> Christ leads me through no darker rooms
>   Than he went through before;
> And he that to God's kingdom comes
>   Must enter by this door.
>
> Come Lord, when grace hath made me meet
>   Thy blessed face to see:
> For if thy work on earth be sweet,
>   What will thy glory be?
>
> My knowledge of that life is small,
>   The eye of faith is dim;
> But 'tis enough that Christ knows all,
>   And I shall be with him
>
> *The Hymnal 1940,* 445

Passing mention needs to be made of JOHN BUNYAN's (1628–1688) *Pilgrim's Progress.* The story, which is very well known, is a kind of medieval morality play, with some affinity to the spiritual warfare described by Scupoli. To the best of our knowledge Bunyan, who was a self-educated, self-appointed itinerant preacher, knew nothing but the Bible, the Book of Common Prayer, and Foxe's *Book of Martyrs,* a compilation of the sufferings of Protestants under Queen Mary (1552–1557), published for the first time in 1563. Bouyer describes *Pilgrim's Progress* as "childish and tedious and has contributed not a little to Puritanism's reputation as being the quintessence of boredom."

Instrumental Images
 Experience of justification by grace through faith (an inward discovery).
 Pietas or piety—obedience to God as father.
 Meditation (a la Baxter).

Terminal Images
 Imputed righteousness.
 Fruito divina.
 Union with the *Ungrund.*
 Sweetness (*Sehnsucht*).
 Betrothal.
 Heart of Christ.

SELECT BIBLIOGRAPHY
Richard Baxter, *A Call to the Unconverted.* Baker Book House, 1976.
———, *A Saint's Everlasting Rest.* Allenson, 1962.
Jacob Boehme, *The Way to Christ,* translated by Peter Erb. Paulist Press, 1978.
John Calvin, *The Piety of John Calvin: An Anthology Illustrative of the Spirituality of the Reformer of Geneva,* edited and translated by Ford Lewis Battles. Pittsburgh Theological Seminary, 1969.
———, "Prayer" in *Institutes,* edited by John Dillenberger, *John Calvin: Selections from his Writings,* pp. 307–317. Westminster, 1954.
Martin Luther, *Letters of Spiritual Counsel,* edited by Theodore G. Tappert. Westminster, 1955.

———, "The Lord's Prayer" in The Large Catechism in the *Book of Concord,* edited by Theodore G. Tappert, pp. 420–436. Muhlenberg Press, 1959.

———, "Sermons on the Catechism: On Prayer" in *Martin Luther; Selections from His Writings,* edited by John Dillenberger, pp. 215–228. Doubleday, 1961.

Francis Rous, *Thede, or Virtues Historie.* B. Franklin, 1966.

Radical Protestantism

I have mentioned the *Schwärmer,* for whom Luther had such contempt. These were the Anabaptists of whom THOMAS MÜNZER (1490–1525) was the initial leader. Generally speaking, they are called "enthusiasts," a kind of person present in the Christian spiritual tradition from the beginning. One need only recall Tertullian (c. 160–c. 120) and Joachim of Fiore (c. 1132–1202) as precursors of Münzer. Enthusiasm means, literally, "God inside" you. The teaching is that the Holy Spirit is speaking directly to the believer. Its sixteenth-century form had a continuity with its medieval roots. It is highly subjective, individualistic, millenarian (the belief that Christ's reign on earth of 1000 years is about to begin) antinomian, anti-institutional (both church and state), and anti-intellectual. It is sectarian, excluding all but the "saved" from its company. It exists today in the way the oppressed, who get little of this world's goods, assure themselves of their personal worth since there is little or no outward sign of anyone else deeming them worthy.

Münzer himself taught that there was the living voice of God in the soul. It is an idea that he apparently got from reading Tauler, whose writings were his constant companion from boyhood. The Anabaptist movement was also influenced by the *Devotio moderna,* particularly in its curtailing of liturgical form to a family setting. (If this begins to sound familiar, it is not surprising.) The Anabaptist as a recognizable collective perished with the fall of their "new Jerusalem," Münzer, in 1535; but enthusi-

asm will live on, arising in recognizable forms sporadically and
influencing other forms of spirituality from time to time.

A principal example of such influence is GEORGE FOX
(1624–1691), the founder of the Society of Friends, or Quakers (a
pejorative and largely untrue "label"). Like the enthusiasts, Fox
believed, as the result of a revelation in 1646, that religious institutions were unnecessary, if not demonic, and that, consequently,
the Reformation had not gone far enough. Fox was also opposed
to dogma. He was an itinerant preacher, a prophet, and a mystic,
whose message, in essence, was that God addresses humanity in
an inner light (note the similarity to Münzer and Tauler before
him). Within each person God has placed a "seed"—the *scintilla
animae*—which only needs to be awakened. This sounds simple,
but Fox was not a simple man. Clearly, he was influenced by
Jacob Boehme, which says enough in itself. For example, like
Boehme he uses the animals (or "beasts") as the image for depraved humanity—an image as old as Christianity, and probably
older. This underlines a certain dualism, implicit in enthusiasm.

Where Fox is different from the enthusiasts is that while he
believed in his teaching that the *new Jerusalem,* the new Church of
the spirit, had finally come, his fellow seekers avoided the excesses of the enthusiasts. There is a solidarity and serenity to his
teaching which we know now in the Society of Friends. Bouyer
describes Fox as a man of genius, who rediscovered the principles
of early monasticism—i.e., to go into the desert and wait on the
Spirit. Rufus Jones, a Friend, says Fox "can be rightly appreciated only as he is seen to be a potent member of an organic
group-life which formed him as much as he formed it." It was
the community that saved Fox's teaching from becoming excessively eccentric and individualistic.

Radical Protestant spirituality is affective. Whether or not it is
kataphatic or apophatic depends on what is being said. There is a
connection in radical Protestantism with quietism, which would
relate it to the apophatic dimension; although it had its influence
over the sentimentality that characterizes much of pietism.

Instrumental Images
    Sectarianism.
    Antinomianism, anti-intellectualism, anti-institutionalism.
    Seed.

Terminal Images
    New Jerusalem.
    Inner voice or inner light.

SELECT BIBLIOGRAPHY
George Fox, *Book of Miracles*. Octagon, 1973.

Pietism

In some ways, pietism lies between classical and radical Protestantism. It is a reaction to the sterile theology of the former, particularly in Germany, and is influenced by the latter. But then again it has a characteristic of its own. As we have already indicated, the *Devotio moderna* was a pietistic movement: a reaction to a sterile theology (nominalism), expressing a generally sentimental, personal, self-congratulatory feeling of God's presence. It is anti-intellectual and often extra-institutional. Pietism's classical expression is derived from PHILLIPP JAKOB SPENER (1635–1705) and his efforts to restore an evangelical fervor in Lutheranism. There is little doubt that we experienced a resurgence of pietism in the 1970s in reaction to the radical theology of the 1960s. Whether this is a third cycle or a recrudescence of classical pietism only history will be able to tell. American religion, where it has lost the rigor of the English Puritans or the theological acumen of Roman Catholic or Anglican thought, has sought to move beyond a civil religion in terms of pietism. It is for this reason that so much space is devoted to what is essentially a shallow form of spirituality.

There are those who disagree both as to our description of pietism and its founder. Some would argue that JOHANN ARNDT (1555–1621) was the founder of German pietism. Like Spener he protested the polemical and petty arguments of the Lutheran theologians and wanted a revival of a doctrine of the spiritual life. He explicitly joined Staupitz (Luther's teacher), the *Devotio moderna,* Tauler, and Bernard in a theology of spirituality. Arndt was ecumenical in spirit and his *True Christianity* was read by all, Protestants, Anglicans, Roman Catholics, and Orthodox. But he was not a Pietist in the technical sense. He had a profound respect for theology and he did not generate conventicles. (Spener claimed Arndt as a predecessor, which may be one reason some insist he founded the movement.) Arndt was interested in the "new life" (which is why Ernest Stoeffler says he was not a mystic, since he did not speak of "union"), but not a new life bought at the price of no intellect. (It would appear that the image of the new life became a dominant one in pietism, particularly in American preaching.) His favorite phrase was, "It is faith that fashions the love of Christ in the faithful heart." And faith for him was an act of thinking and will as well as feeling.

It may be that we are debating the definition of a word, because Stoeffler in *The Rise of Evangelical Pietism* sees pietism as declining with Spener. What is described here, with the general understanding of historians, as pietism is, however, just what Spener and his followers taught: an Evangelical spirituality that appropriates Calvin's use of the *Devotio moderna* without any appreciation for his development of John Gerson's *pietas.* In other words, pietism is really not "pietism," it is "devotionalism" at its subjective and sentimental worst. The name, pietism, comes, however, from a group that met in Spener's house, called the *collegia pietatis,* "the college of piety" (note that the very name is derived from a "conventicle," which should, again, have resonance for us today). Spener himself admitted that the *collegia pietatis* soon developed illuministic—i.e., a belief that the Holy Spirit has spoken to the individual directly—and pharisaical tendencies. It was fideistic to the core.

Spener's work generated a tradition within Lutheranism of lay spiritual direction, based on the continuing tradition—from

Aelred through Anselm, the Dominicans, and Francis de Sales—
of the spiritual friendship. This was also picked up by Wesley.
Unfortunately, it did not prevail in the general order of things,
and one finds in evangelical Christianity to this date a kind of
"do-it-yourself spirituality."

AUGUST HERMANN FRANCKE (1663–1727), an associate of
Spener but not a disciple, introduced the notion of conversion as
the sole guarantee of saving faith. ("Conversion" differs from "illumination," as in George Fox's experience of revelation, in that
the Holy Spirit effects a change in nature or outlook. Illumination indicates only a raised or expanded consciousness.) This is of
immeasurable importance for the subsequent influence of pietism,
particularly when it is combined with a Calvinist theology of predestination (which is not characteristic of Lutheranism). How do
we know we are elect? It is by some *felt consolation.*

This leads to the brief discussion of one of America's greatest
theologians, JONATHAN EDWARDS (1705–1758). Some remember
Edwards as the author of hell-fire sermons, particularly "Sinners
in the Hands of an Angry God." He epitomizes the rock-ribbed
Calvinist. But he was much more than this. What Edwards
taught was *pietas* when American religion was already moving
toward moralism. (Moralism is an exaggerated emphasis on religion as "character building" and fails to understand the fundamental contradiction in the human will, in regard to both sin
and the good intention. Essentially it ends up offering pious plat-
itudes to humans drowning in their sin.) *Pietas,* we need to
remember, was an attitude of obedience to God as the all-power-
ful father. Pietism was to sentimentalize this notion, which then
became part of American moralism. God became the kindly
grandfather, whom we can expect to satisfy our every whim. This
was not Edwards' teaching.

Edwards did believe, however, that there was in the being of
man a yearning for God, a belief that is rooted in Gregory of
Nyssa and Origen. He went on to say that God plants a seed in
humanity, which he then "waters" so that a person grows to

union with Christ. We become aware of this *by the affection of our hearts*. At this point we need to be very careful, because Edwards was a man of very subtle intellect. Whether or not he believed in a consolation in terms of conversion by rule is uncertain and he seems to have been open to a variety of religious experiences, so one must not simply conclude that Edwards was a Pietist teaching the necessity of some sentimental consolations. He was not. But he was instrumental in bringing GEORGE WHITEFIELD (1714–1770) to America, which instigated the First Great Awakening and the beginning of *revivalism*. Revivalism, bereft of Puritan rationalism, became the principal instrument of American pietism. Revivalism can be identified with American frontier religion, the "camp meeting," Charles Finney, Dwight Moody, Billy Sunday, Billy Graham, prohibition, outlawing of prostitution, sodomy laws, etc.

Another important figure in American spirituality, who with Edwards needs to be seen as related to but separate from pietism, is JOHN WOOLMAN (1720–1772). Woolman was a "recommended minister" in the Society of Friends—the Quakers did not have ordained clergy—who spent thirty years of his ministry as an itinerant preacher. His *Journal* is a record of his travels. The style of the *Journal* is typical of an eighteenth and nineteenth century literary genre, and is very reminiscent of John Wesley's journals. It is a simple account of his day to day travels as a preacher in rural America, describing people and places as seen through the eyes of evangelical piety.

What is particularly striking in Woolman is the combination of mystical awareness and social concern found in his *Journal*. Woolman believed that God spoke through dreams and visions. He had a deep sense of God's divine providence, directing him in the smallest kind of detail. He had read *The Imitation of Christ,* Jacob Boehme, and William Law, and so was familiar with that tradition of piety. At the same time, he was deeply opposed to slavery and left an abiding influence on the American abolitionist movement. He was also opposed to war. As Woolman put it, "I was fully convinced that the proceedings in wars are inconsistent with the purity of the Christian religion."

We need to contrast with Edwards and Woolman LUDWIG GRAF VON ZINZENDORF (1700–1760), the "godfather" of the Moravians or the United Brethren. Zinzendorf's theology is very simple, if one can call it a theology: Keep the heart away from the head and believe with all your heart. He could not see why all Christians could not unite around the heart and forget the differences of the head. Zinzendorf engaged in several romantic adventures in the name of Christ. A German nobleman, he was able to help the Moravians in various establishments—Herrnhut, Georgia, Herrntag; London; etc. In Georgia he came into contact with John Wesley.

Zinzendorf's teaching was highly sentimental. God the Father was *Papa*, the Holy Spirit was *Mama*, and Jesus was *Bruder* (brother) or *Lämmlein* ("lambkins"). He was fascinated by the blood from the side of Christ. His hymns reeked of it. Out of over two thousand hymns he wrote, the two found in *The Hymnal 1940* (411 and 425) are, by far, among the more chastened. All husbands, he taught, were really vice-husbands, since every woman's real husband was Christ. While the Puritans were quite content for marital sex to be good fun, Zinzendorf even disapproved of intercourse in marriage—adding to the guilty conscience of the American Protestant. He wanted all his followers to become "little children," which meant that they were to be childish or silly instead of childlike.

Zinzendorf, despite his obvious sincerity and love of Christ, exemplifies where pietism can lead. It can become sick, especially if it does not have the corrective of a rigorous theological thought. JOHN WESLEY (1703–1791; Feast day: March 3) is the example of someone, who, while influenced by Zinzendorf—not to mention William Law, Ignatius Loyola, the *Imitation of Christ*, Teresa of Avila, Francis de Sales, Fenelon, and Jakob Boehme— had the intellect to redeem many of the pietist insights. Wesley lived and died an Anglican priest, who said his daily Office and was dedicated to the sacraments. He was a child of his age and was in the pietist tradition, but he was not an enthusiast. As he describes his experience of conversion: "In the event I went unwillingly to a society [Moravian] on Aldersgate Street, where one was reading Luther's Preface to the Epistle to the Romans. About a quarter before nine, while he was reading the change which God works in the heart through faith in Christ, I felt my heart strangely warmed." This experience has become the "cornerstone" to Methodist mysticism. For Wesley it is a prophetic mysticism.

Wesley was no Calvinist. He opposed, to the last, George Whitefield's preoccupation with predestination. He had a deep commitment to justification by grace through faith, but his belief in the sanctifying presence of the Holy Spirit lay well within the tradition of classical Christian spirituality. Salvation for Wesley was both "instantaneous and gradual." He taught the notion that we should have an awareness of "growing on to perfection." The three steps to perfection for Wesley are: 1) justification 2) redemption, and 3) sanctification.

John Wesley believed that by *preaching* he could bring to a largely indifferent England—and, incidently, America as well— the same experience of God's presence he had in his conversion. He is a transition figure for our purposes because he saw himself doing this in a world torn loose from its roots by the industrial revolution; his spirituality is almost contemporary, as we shall see. His divergence from Anglican doctrine seems to come in the area of his priorities. His first priority was to preach the Gospel. It was the intransigence of the Church of England that forced his followers out and we get the distinction between "chapel" (the pietist conventicle) and "church" (the liturgy of the established church). In many ways, however, Wesley was more Catholic than the Church of England.

For anyone wanting to experience the highly kataphatic and very affective piety of John Wesley and his brother Charles we need only turn to his many hymns. In fact the Wesleys perfected the art of *hymnody* as a spiritual discipline.

Wesley, like Edwards, was no pietist. Edwards' theology could be misread to give comfort to pietist spirituality; and Wesley, influenced by the pietists, begot a movement which, when it came to this country and lost its intellectual roots, fluctuated between pietism and civil religion. The problem with pietism is that it confused piety with theology. A good corrective to pietism would be either Edwards or Wesley or, better, both. For Wesley was always against the pietists, as well as the quietists, including Law. The difference between him and William Law can be charted in this manner.

	Law	*Wesley*
Focus	individual	society
Action	renunciation	service
Goal	hereafter	present

Instrumental Images
Conversion-felt consolation.
Pietism.
Affection of our hearts.
Revivalism.
To become childish.
Hymnody.

Terminal Images
New life.

SELECT BIBLIOGRAPHY
Johann Arndt, *True Christianity.* Paulist, 1979.
Jonathan Edwards, *Works.* Yale, 1959–1977.
Jakob Spener, *Pia desideria,* translated by Theodore G. Tappert. Fortress, 1974.
John Wesley, *Devotions and Prayers.* Baker Book House, 1977.
John Woolman, *The Journal and Major Essays,* edited by Phillips P. Moultin, Oxford, 1971.

Sparks Among the Stubble

The purpose of this section is to show that while the late eighteenth and the entire nineteenth and early twentieth centuries were singularly undistinguished for a concerted witness to the spiritual life, there were some exceptions to the rule. The Industrial Revolution, a growing secularism, and an almost unchecked sentimentality in Christian thinking seemed to encourage only the worst in spirituality. Who stood against the tide?

The evolution of capitalism, which made possible a consumer society, eventually brought our culture to a blatant, mindless hedonism, which has made asceticism seem only stupid, particularly in the face of a disenchanted expectation of experience. "If it feels good, do it" is the inevitable ultimate banality in a society that believes "you only go around once."

Mysticism, with its emphasis upon the receptive mode of consciousness, seemed far too feminine to the patriarchal culture of the nineteenth and early twentieth centuries. Albrech Ritschl's (1822–1889) deep distrust of mysticism, which epitomizes the intellectual climate of Protestantism toward spirituality after Kant, is more a rationale for a masculine prejudice than an original argument. His understanding of classical Christian mysticism is a caricature, a "straw man" to attack, not a critical analysis of the historical reality. But he spoke for many people.

Gerhard Tersteegen (1697–1769), a Dutchman, a Protestant, and a contemporary of Wesley, is a true mystical theologian. He is deeply rooted in the Bible. God's word makes its impression upon the person's soul, but that impression is *not* made in feeling. It is made in the *nous* (as in Evagrius) or the mind (The German word is *Vernunft*.) The mind is a sleeping power, and when the Holy Spirit awakens it the person is given over to a *contemplative intuition* of the Word. This leads to an awareness of God's presence in us. Like St. John of the Cross, Tersteegen is deeply suspicious of "spiritual phenomena," which can lead to illusion. He is also criticlal of "faith in one's faith" or "faith as a good work," which is a problem for Protestantism. There is a healthy intuition/intellect marriage in his teaching.

We know Tersteegen largely through his hymns. For example,

God himself is with us;
  Let us all adore him,
And with awe appear before him.
  God is here within us;   ·
Soul, in silence fear him,
  Humbly, fervently draw near him.
Now his own Who have known
  God, in worship lowly,
Yield their spirits wholly.

The Hymnal 1940, 477, 1st stanza

Those words bespeak his sense of the immediacy of God, if we but attend to his Word and his presence. This apprehension of God to the intuitive person is central to an authentic Christian spirituality.

Bouyer says that Tersteegen is the last of the Protestant spiritual masters. In Anglicanism the story is no better. The English evangelicals, being with William Wilberforce, are compassionate do-gooders, but no spiritual giants. The Tractarians are equally uninspiring. John Keble (Feast day: March 29) is sweet, but limited. Edward Pusey (Feast day: September 18) is erudite, arrogant, and boring. John Henry Newman was an original theologian, but as Friederich von Hügel, himself no mean student of Christian spirituality, once observed, Newman was incapable of ending a sermon, or a poem on anything but a note of gloom. Thornton has a telling observation. "These Tractarian pastors proved past masters at doing the right things for the wrong reasons, frequently in the wrong order."

Roman Catholicism was in the doldrums. JEAN-BAPTISTE MARIE VIANNEY (1786–1859), known as the Curé d'Ars, a deserter from the French army and a seminary failure; and THERESE OF LISIEUX (1873–1897), a childlike Carmelite nun; are typical of the best piety of the period. The Curé d'Ars was a great confessor, a faithful priest of the people, who had an abiding horror of sin. He counseled a simple gospel of love. He is the patron saint of parish priests!

Therese, who died at twenty-four of tuberculosis, was a saint of the people. She is copatronness of France with Joan of Arc. Her simple self-sacrifice gave the average believer a hope for perfection. She is known as the "Little Flower" from the subtitle in the English version of her autobiography, *The Story of a Soul,* as well as her promise, "I shall come to make the darkness a flood of roses." The stereotype of Therese as only saccharine is unjust, however, and there is a reappraisal of her witness underway.

The thing to note about both the Curé d'Ars and Therese is their popularity among the people. The nineteenth century and first half of the twentieth century was a time for populism ("political pietism"). Populism can be demonic in the extreme, as with Hitler or Lenin, or just "moderately evil" as with Huey Long. It can also work to the good, depending on who the "savior" is. It works through mass hysteria. Its lability is due to its lack of intellectual substance.

A Roman Catholic, who was every inch an intellect and no man of the people, but needs to be mentioned, is GERALD MANLEY HOPKINS (1844–1889). Hopkins was an Englishman and a Jesuit. He was also a poet and a man before his time. His poetry, which can be difficult and should be read aloud, sought to give expression to that intuition of God's presence within the phenomena, which is *the* problem for postcritical (i.e., after Immanuel Kant) ascetical and mystical theology. Hopkins speaks of perceiving the "inscape" as opposed to the "landscape" of things. In this sense he is related to Tersteegen's contemplative intuition, Edmund Husserl's apprehension, or what Paul Ricouer in the present times calls "second naïvete." It is to know the subject beyond the objects of our experience by a willful act of the knowing subject.

Still another Roman Catholic worthy of mention was FRIEDERICH VON HÜGEL (1852–1925), a married layman, who because of his commitment to biblical criticism and his friendship with Roman Catholic "modernists" was more followed outside Roman Catholic circles than inside. Deaf from the age of eighteen, the son of a Scottish Presbyterian woman turned Roman Catholic, von Hügel lived from the age of fifteen in England. He was a philosopher and theologian who was much ahead of his time—despite a certain narrowness of perspective common to the Victorian mind. His spirituality is open, ambiguous, intuitive, and, above all, incarnational. It focused on the Spirit enfleshed in history united to the spirit of humanity. Joseph Whelan, the author of *The Spirituality of Friederich von Hügel,* has described von Hügel's purpose as the "civilizing of spirituality and the spiritualizing of civilization." Von Hügel rejected both pietism and secularism, but was himself thoroughly *secular and deeply religious.*

In 1920 he wrote to a young Anglican woman, age seventeen, who was about to be confirmed. In this letter he defines "four great religious principles and practices," which sum up his spirituality. They have a very "Anglican feel," despite his Roman Catholicism. They are:

> 1) the reality and practice of the presence of God . . . the cultivation of the sense . . . of his prevenience. . . . 2) the reality and practice of contingency, of creatureliness. . . . we have a body. . . . 3) the reality, and practice of the sense of, our human weakness, error, sin. . . . Human nature is *not* essentially violated, and the whole of religion does *not* consist in a sense of sin. . . . Yet it is also true that . . . we *are* responsible. . . . 4) The reality, and the sense of the true function, of suffering . . . to accept it, and gently to utilize it towards loving God and man.

There was an impressive revival of orthodox spirituality, beginning with the Greek Church, in the latter part of the eighteenth century. NICODEMUS OF THE HOLY MOUNTAIN (1748–1809) was the leader of this movement. He combined a zeal for the revival of Byzantine spirituality in the spirit of Evagrius, which was captured in his book, *Philokalia* (literally "the love of beautiful things"), with a catholic spirit in an ascetical method, epitomized by his translation of Scupoli's *Spiritual Combat*. Nicodemus had a deep appreciation for the participation of the whole person, body and soul, in the act of contemplation. He also pushes for an interior recitation of the Jesus Prayer as the prayer of the spirit and the heart.

This revival of orthodox spirituality brought attention to what is called "astonishment of soul," a mystical term for the sudden affective expansion of our horizons of knowledge. It is important for many reasons, not the least of which is the relation of this concept of the "imaginative shock" that Ray Hart, a contemporary theologian, argues is intrinsic to fundamental theology. This points to the relation between prayer and theologiclal recollection or, as the Victorines put it, the symbolic perception of the created order.

One last "spark" that needs to be mentioned is the prototypical figure in the Russian Orthodox spiritual revival of the nineteenth century. This is THEOPHAN THE RECLUSE (1815–1894). It is said of Theophan that one cannot understand Russian Orthodoxy unless one understands him. A bishop, an anchorite, a highly educated man, he spent the last years of his life seeing no one, but writing many letters. He is steeped in the Fathers, but was a man familiar with his times.

The heart of Theophan's teaching is summed up in his own words. "The principal thing is to stand with the mind in the heart before God, and to go on standing before Him unceasingly day and night, until the end of life." For Theophan and the Hesychasts a human person is four things: body, soul, spirit, and heart. The heart encompasses the other three and is the organ of prayer. This is a monistic notion of what it is to be a human.

The spiritual ascent for Theophan is in four stages:
1. The prayer of the lips or verbal prayer.
2. The prayer of the mind or thinking about God.
3. The prayer of the mind in the heart, or focusing the mind in the heart so that at one point God takes over.

4. The prayer of the heart or the soul as captive of the spirit of prayer.
   a) The soul sees everything and is in control.
   b) The soul is in ecstasy and is ravished so that it forgets itself and has no control.

Theophan is the principal channel for the interpretation of hesychasm and the prayer of the heart to our times. One cannot pray just in the head, he says. My translation of this would be that we need to pray in the receptive mode of consciousness or with intuition and not just in the action mode or with thinking. The Jesus Prayer is the most immediate instrument of this form of prayer, which is still known in only limited ways in contemporary Western Christian spirituality. Theophan said this of the Jesus Prayer.

> The Jesus Prayer is like any other prayer. It is stronger than all other prayers only in virtue of the all-powerful Name of Jesus, Our Lord and Savior. But it is necessary to invoke His Name with a full and unwavering faith—with a deep certainty that He is near. . . . The Jesus Prayer is not some talisman. Its power comes from faith in the Lord, and from a deep union of the mind and heart with Him.

In other words, transcendental meditation as a method of relaxation is not the "same thing" as the Jesus Prayer.

Probably the most immediate access that a contemporary American would have to the revival of orthodox spirituality is the book *The Way of the Pilgrim,* which is a biographical exposition of the Jesus Prayer. In a way it is a Russian *Pilgrim's Progress,* only better.

Finally, it would be remiss for us not to call attention to an Anglican woman who lurks in the memory of Episcopalians over fifty, EVELYN UNDERHILL (1875–1941). A pupil of Von Hügel, she was an author, retreat conductor, and translator, whose commitment to the mystical tradition kept it alive in Anglicanism between the two World Wars. Underhill was not herself an origi-

nal thinker or a mystic. She was a synthesizer. Her theology, as
that of other Anglican worthies of the time between the two
World Wars—e.g., F. P. Harton and Bede Frost—is indicative
of the end of an era and is now outdated. Underhill's understanding of Christian spirituality was rooted in Olier's three
themes: adoration, communion, and cooperation. Her belief that
adoration constituted the soul of prayer had more influence on
Episcopal confirmation classes in the 1930s and 1940s than anything else she said. Prayer is, then, the acknowledgment that the
reality in the final analysis is the intimate presence of God to humanity. Her goal was to enable us to discover this for ourselves.

Instrumental Images
    Contemplative intuition.
    Secular and deeply religious.
    Astonishment of soul.
    Adoration, communion, cooperation.

Terminal Images
    Inscape.

SELECT BIBLIOGRAPHY

The Art of Prayer: An Orthodox Anthology, translated by E. Kadlou-
    bovsky and E. M. Palmer. Faber and Faber, 1966.
Gerard Manley Hopkins, *Poems and Prose.* Penguin, 1953.
Friederich von Hügel, *Mystical Elements of Religion.* 2 vols. Attic
    Press, 1961.
———, *Spiritual Counsels and Letters.* Harper, 1964.
Gerhard Tersteegen, selections in a biography by H. E. Govan,
    1898.
Therese of Lisieux, *Story of a Soul.* Christian Classics, 1975.
The Evelyn Underhill Reader, edited by T. S. Kepler. 1962.
The Way of the Pilgrim, translated by R. M. French. Harper,
    1952.

The Contemporary Scene

The closer one comes to his own time the more risky is his judgment. Therefore, to single out the spiritual masters of the last fifty years is arbitrary at best and one does so only with a willingness for the list to be amended.

It would seem that the West is experiencing a revolution in consciousness which has an inevitable effect upon Christian spirituality that is just as significant as the rise of Neo-Platonism in the third century. (Please note that while the Aristotelian revolution in the thirteenth century and the Kantian revolution in the eighteenth century changed fundamental and systematic theology in each instance, neither significantly effected ascetical and mystical theology, which has remained Neo-Platonic until the twentieth century.) Whereas the primary definition of the distinctive nature of humanity today remains consciousness—i.e., *nous* or mind—and consequently consciousness is still the central focus of Christian spirituality, we are coming to realize that mind is ontologically social and incarnate. We *are* our community and we *are* our body.

"Where is the presence, where is the glory of God to be found?" asks the contemporary Jewish mystic, Abraham Heschel. He answers himself: "It is found in the world, . . . in the Bible, and in a sacred deed." Dag Hammarskjöld, of whom we shall say more shortly, put it more succinctly. "In our era, the road to holiness necessarily passes through the world of action." We must not think that this is an altogether novel idea. The twelfth and thirteenth centuries particularly knew this, as we see in someone like Francis or Dominic. The centrality of this worldly asceticism, however, is unique to our times. It seems to be characteristic of every contemporary Christian spiritual master.

Not so developed is the realization that the body is involved. A satisfying spirituality of sexuality, which is not tinged by a simplisitc *apatheia,* is yet to be written. Perhaps it will emerge in the next generation. Certainly the presence of genital arousal in spiritual experience is common and needs to be acknowledged as a positive element—rather than repressed and made a subject of embarrassment. A spirituality of sexuality, including genitality, may not come from a northern European male. We are culturally retarded in regard to our sexuality. Martin Luther King could have written a sex-positive spirituality. Possibly there are other non-white males or women who can transcend the controversies of the moment and can gain sufficient distance in the presence of God to speak to our androgyny before God.

But who are some contemporary spiritual masters of whom we already know? We must begin with SIMONE WEIL (1909–1943). Weil was a Jew, who believed herself a Christian and Roman Catholic, although she refused baptism because of her desire to identify with the unbelievers. She also had a wide-ranging taste in authors, not all of them Christian by any means. She was brought to Christianity through visits to a Portuguese fishing village, to Assisi, and to Solesmes in France to witness the glory of the liturgy. George Herbert's poetry, as I said before, had a profound influence on her. She suffered great physical pain, which sharpened her sensitivities and gave her an intense identification with the poor and the suffering. It is not surprising that her spirituality places the Passion of Christ as central. This gives her a common bond with the Franciscans and Julian of Norwich.

During World War II she was a French freedom fighter. She left France during the war and came to England. Yet she would only eat as she believed her countrymen suffering in France ate. Weakened by her fast, she exacerbated her chronic ill health and died at the age of thirty-four. She was a mystic, experiencing God in an immediate way. But Weil believed that such an experience required waiting (*hypomene*)—maybe for a lifetime—for God in affliction. But unlike Samuel Beckett's play, "Waiting for Godot," which ends in emptiness and is reminiscent of her sense of the absence of God, she found God speaking in response to her waiting. It is no surprise that Meister Eckhart and John of the Cross were among Weil's favorite spiritual writers.

Affliction makes God appear to be absent for a time, more absent than a dead man, more absent than light in the utter darkness of a cell. A kind of horror submerges the whole soul. During this absence there is nothing to love. What is terrible is that if, in this darkness where there is nothing to love, the Soul ceases to love, God's absence becomes final. The soul has to go on loving in the emptiness, or at least to go on wanting to love, though it may be with an infinitesimal part of itself. Then, one day, God will come to show himself to the soul and to reveal the beauty of the world to it, as in the case of Job. But if the soul stops loving it falls, even in this life, into something almost equivalent to hell.

The spirituality of Simone Weil cuts directly through the cant of pietism. While she has a great love of beauty, it is not an emotional or romantic notion. The beauty she admires is ascertained with the mind and the order of necessity. She was a well-read and thoughtful person who lived not by feeling but by will. Weil's spirituality stands over against the institution. She had a strong suspicion of all structures, born of observing what National Socialism had done in Germany. She is an existentialist in the tradition of Kierkegaard and Dostoevski. She tends to be apophatic and speculative.

No less unlikely a candidate for spiritual honors is DAG HAMMARSKJÖLD (1905–1961), the son of a Swedish prime minister, a banker, statesman, and ultimately Secretary-General of the United Nations. A member of a state church and a very private man, his single contribution to the history of Christian spirituality was a personal journal, found in his apartment after his tragic death. Its title was *Markings.* What makes Hammarskjöld remarkable is that, in spite of himself, his vocation was probably that of a mystic, although he reveals much of the Lutheran prejudice against mysticism. His political life was ultimately an avocation.

To be sure, he read the fourteenth-century German and English mystics, as well as John of the Cross. He opens his journal with a quotation from Meister Eckhart, "Only the hand that erases can write the true thing." The generally short, epigrammatic statements that constitute his writing are laced with other citations from Christian authors, including Swedish hymns. His writing is not terribly original or incisive, but remarkable for the fact of who he was.

Death and the cross are a central theme throughout. In 1950 he wrote, "At least he knew this much about himself—I know what man is—his vulgarity, lust, pride, envy—and longing. Longing—among other things, for the Cross." In 1951 he says, "Committed to the future—even if that only means '*se preparer à bien mourir*' [to prepare oneself to die well]." In 1953 he apparently had some kind of religious experience, summed up in the short sentence, "Not I, but God in me."

After that his entries are more prolix and overtly Christian. Everyone would have his own favorites. I share a few of mine here.

> The only kind of dignity which is genuine is that which is not diminished by the indifference of others.

> That piece of pagan anthromorphism: the belief that, in order to educate us, God wishes us to suffer. How far from this is the assent to suffering when it strikes us *because* we have obeyed what we have seen to be God's will.

> Humility is just as much the opposite of self-abasement as it is of self-exaltation. To be humble is *not to make comparisons.* . . . To have humility is to experience reality, not *in relation to ourselves,* but in its sacred independence.

Hammarskjöld was a kind of twentieth-century sage, fluctuating from the banal and obvious observation of a man seeking meaning in a confused world to an insight born of unceasing prayer that arrests our attention and opens a vew vista. He was kataphatic and speculative.

In contrast to Hammerskjöld, but yet as a strange complement, there is THOMAS MERTON (1915–1968). In a paper on

Marxism and monasticism which he delivered the day of his death in Bangkok, where, among other reasons, he had gone to enter into dialogue with Buddhist monasticism, Merton wrote: "The monk is essentially someone who takes up a critical attitude toward the world and its structures." Yet he believed that "the way to relevance was the way of prayer and contemplation." Merton revealed the fundamental lie of all who think the mystical way is an escape from reality.

Merton was born an Episcopalian and found the Episcopal Church spiritually shallow. He became a Roman Catholic and a Cistercian monk. His life was a quest for solitude, and in this desert he came to know evil for what it is and to know humanity for what it can be. Merton has a remarkable ability to cut through the cant and posturing of our age. Yet he wanted above all to be contemplative, which he defines as one who "makes use of all the resources of theology and philosophy and art and music in order to focus a simple affective gaze on God." This is not unrelated to Weil's "waiting." Merton was generally kataphatic and speculative, although he advocated the apophatic approach.

Quietism, Merton believed, is the "complete contradiction" of Christian contemplation. Christian contemplation seeks the perfection of love, which inevitably leads to action. In speaking of the difference between a good and bad meditation, Merton wrote,

> All methods of meditation that are, in effect, merely devices for allaying and assuaging the experience of emptiness and dread are ultimately evasions which can do nothing to help us. . . . What we need is not a false peace which enables us to evade the implacable light of judgement, but the grace courageously to accept the bitter truth that is revealed to us; to abandon our inertia, our egotism and submit entirely to the demands of the Spirit. . . .

He goes on to speak of the "impenetrable self-assurance of the Pharisee," and its false " 'goodness'."

Such "goodness" is preserved by routine and the habitual avoidance of serious risk—indeed of serious challenge. In order to avoid apparent evil, this pseudo-goodness will ignore the summons of genuine good. It will prefer routine duty to courage and creativity. In the end it will be content with established procedures and safe formulas, while turning a blind eye to the greatest enormities of injustice and uncharity.

Merton took traditional concepts, such as purity of heart, and made of them the basis for a very contemporary concern for God's world. "Prayer does not blind us to the world," he wrote, "but it transforms our vision of the world." His piety was in the Cistercian tradition; he was a contemplative, but he discerned God's presence in the world and was therefore able to take great risks.

A black Southern Baptist preacher, MARTIN LUTHER KING (1929–1968) had little of the long tradition of Western European Christian spirituality in his heritage. He studied the Protestant mystics, however, and not only influenced by Walter Rauschenbush and the Social Gospel, as well as the personalism of Edgar Brightman and Harold deWolf at Boston University, but he was deeply touched by the writings of Mohandas Ghandi, the great Hindu mystic and revolutionary. All of this was filtered through the consciousness of a black, Southern intellectual. The effect was to create a charismatic leader, who understood the demonic power of sin but who changed a society by means of a vision born of prayer.

The terminal image for King was the *beloved community*. The power of that vision was, perhaps, best spelled out at the Lincoln Memorial in 1963 in the famous speech, "I have a dream!" In his own words his dream was

When we let freedom ring, when we let it ring from every village and every hamlet, and every state and every city, we will be able to speed up that day when all God's children, black men and white men, Jews and Gentiles, Protestants and

> Catholics, will be able to join hands and sing in the words of
> that old Negro spiritual, "Free at last! Free at last! Thank
> God Almighty, we are free at last!"

King's piety was kataphatic and affective, obviously. It was not
sentimental, however. The use of nonviolence to protest injustice
required the greatest possible spiritual depth.

> Only through an inner spiritual transformation do we gain
> the strength to fight vigorously the evils of the world in a
> humble and loving spirit. The transformed nonconformist,
> moreover, never yields to the passive sort of patience which is
> an excuse to do nothing.

In his own way King had a great deal in common with Merton.
True awareness of God's presence called forth the courage to risk
in behalf of the self-revelation of God and the vision that engen-
ders.

This vision also gives a kind of peace—the kind that William
Alexander Percy called "strife closed in the sod" (*The Hymnal
1940*, 437)—which is the assurance of God's blessing. These are
the words of a mystic, who intuits that his time has come to die.

> Well, I don't know what will happen now, but it really
> doesn't matter with me now. Because I've been to the moun-
> tain top. I won't mind. Like anybody, I would like to live a
> long life. Longevity has its place. But I'm not concerned
> about that now. I just want to do God's will. And He's
> allowed me to go up to the mountain. And I've looked over,
> and I've seen the promised land.
>
> I may not get there with you, but I want you to know to-
> night that we as a people will get the promised land. So I'm
> happy tonight. I'm not worried about anything. I'm not fear-
> ing any man. "Mine eyes have seen the glory of the coming of
> the Lord."

The next day he was assassinated.

It is worthy of notice that the four contemporary Christian

spiritual masters I have chosen all died in an unusual manner, which can be interpreted as a witness to the God they knew in prayer and served in the world.

Instrumental Images
  Worldly asceticism.
  Waiting.
  Affliction.
  Attentive gaze.
  Nonviolent protest.

Terminal Images
  The beloved community.

SELECT BIBLIOGRAPHY

Dag Hammarskjöld, *Markings,* translated by Leif Sjöberg and W. H. Auden. Knopf, 1964.

The writings of Martin Luther King all possess a sense of his spirituality and, at the same time, we still wait for an edition of his speeches which will be the ideal source.

Thomas Merton, *Contemplative Prayer.* Image Books, 1971.
———, *Life and Holiness.* Doubleday, n.d.
———, *Mystics and Zen Masters.* Dell, 1969.
———, *New Seeds of Contemplation.* New Directions, 1972.
Simone Weil, *Waiting for God,* translated by Emma Craufurd. Harper Torchbooks, n.d.

Conclusion

How does one appropriate for oneself over two thousand years of the sense a tradition has made of the experience of prayer? This analysis is a brief attempt to assist us in "getting our minds around" the variety and complexity of Christian spirituality, and the result cannot be resolved in a few simple answers. The solution does not lie in discerning some single pattern within the genius of so many spiritual masters, although there is a recurrence of images within the kaleidoscope of authentic Christian spirituality, which is rooted in the common human experience of transcendence. The end product of this survey is more like a materials list for building a life of prayer, with the blueprint emerging as the individual explores his or her inner self.

We are all beginners in prayer, and we all have to begin with the experience of prayer. Do not expect any book, much less a compressed historical summary to be the substitute for action. This analysis can, however, do two things. First, it can save us from a shallow or doctrinaire notion as to the nature of Christian spirituality. There are times in the past when the saints teach us to avoid the sentimentality of our romantic age, as well as its low tolerance to ignorance and ambiguity.

Second, this analysis can give us a variety of names for the means and the end of prayer. There is a freedom in identifying what is to be expected and what we have experienced. The many images lead beyond the Spirit enfleshed in history to the ineffable God who transcends all our names and yet makes himself known to us. We can develop our own spiritual theology, without considering it definitive, and be challenged at the same time to move deeper by the power of God into the hiddenness of God. What shape it takes will vary with each of us.

In the planning stage of this book, many academically-minded Christians were asked what in the writing of the spiritual masters strikes them as particularly important for their lives now. The theme that embraces all else is the *journey*. As Christians we have a journey before us and we need to get on with it. The fact of the journey's existence is reason enough for undertaking it. It does not have to have an ulterior purpose. Living is making the journey of the spirit. To avoid that journey is only to exist.

Two images, the mountain and the desert, stand out as characteristic of the terrain over which the journey leads us. There is in the first image the constant rehearsal of the ascent—as the ascent of Mt. Carmel in John of the Cross—toward union or perfection.

In the second image we are reminded that purity of mind and poverty of spirit are required. Both images emphasize the danger or risk in the spiritual journey. The risk cannot be avoided. One must be willing to fight the demons as well as be served by the angels. Furthermore, there is no obvious identification of the demons as compared with the angels.

The importance of discretion or discernment is crucial, therefore. Except for individuals such as Richard of St. Victor or Ignatius Loyola, the question of discernment remains relatively undeveloped. It is a subject which needs careful explication. Discernment is not an alternative to risk, but is the ability of the one who undertakes the spiritual journey with all its dangers.

Darkness is an important and ambiguous presence in our reading of the spiritual masters. Some, such as Gregory of Nyssa, speak of it as a positive presence; others, such as John of the Cross, refer to it as a necessary negative presence. Contemporary people respond to the presence, positive or negative, of a darkness in the spiritual life. This awareness of the darkness, along with the risk of sensible spirituality, is a clue to the renewed concern for spiritual direction in ministry today.

Yet it is important to see that there is encouragement in the spiritual masters and not just words of warnings. Those persons with whom I have studied the mystics comment again and again that there are those flashes of insight, those moments of grace, where we are deeply aware of God's presence. There is a key scriptural verse for many Christians who have gone before which speaks to us with freshness. "I know a man in Christ," Paul writes," who fourteen years ago was caught up to the third heaven—whether in the body or out of the body I do not know, God knows" (II Cor. 12.2). There is the promise of the ecstatic experience that illumines all that follows.

It is essential that we not try to "codify"—to "make three booths" (Mk. 9:5)—the experience as a way of holding on to it for ourselves and to test the spirituality of others. The tendency in recent years of renewal movements to degenerate into literalism—an institutionalization of the experience of God at the propositional level—is destructive of the very renewal for which we all strive. There is no permanent resting place; no one has captured the ineffable God in his or her formulae; perfection lies in the desire for God, not in the accomplishment of the union. This is why we who have searched the spiritual masters together conclude that we must never lose that delicate balance between the intuitive and the logical, between the receptive mode and the action mode of consciousness.

This is not to say that there are not guidelines along the journey. For us this is the *Christ as the Lord of Creation*. Spiritual theology lays great emphasis upon the Cross, but that emphasis is always against the background of the conviction that humanity was made for union with God. Where the extreme asceticism of Neo-Platonism is tempered, that sense of the cosmos to which we are invited catches up the material world as well. Forensic notions of the Passion of Christ, stemming from Anselm of Canterbury, are mercifully few in the spiritual tradition. But there is a christocentric piety, particularly in the West, from the eleventh and twelfth centuries.

Furthermore, the relation of contemplation to action is expressed in the spiritual pilgrimage as an emptying of self for the other. There is no question but that *theoria* leads to *praxis*, illumination to doing, holiness to virtue.

Anyone who reads the spiritual masters with an open mind is also profoundly impressed by the place of the Scriptures. Christian spirituality in all ages is biblical spirituality. Our forefathers were not higher critics. But neither were they ignorant or literalists. The imagination is freed to draw from the text what illumination it may in accord with the principles of classical rhetoric. We, as contemporary readers, need to affirm the central role of higher criticism, but we can find much profit in a symbolic or anagogical reading when done with intention, with what Paul Ricouer describes as a "second naïvete."

There seems to be a reluctance on the part of many of us to get on with the journey. We read the masters with hesitance and are often surprised to find them fascinating. Why the reluctance or hesitance? Is it possible that we fear we might indeed hear a call from God that summons us from our comfortable place, from our Ur of the Chaldees, to go serve him? It has been said that we need to be careful about what we pray for: we might get it. It should be added that we need to beware, for if we listen to God we might hear him, and what he says may well make us uncomfortable. But it can also make us whole.

Index of Names

Abelard, Peter, 68
Aelred of Rievaulx, 59, 68, 118, 138
Albert the Great, 68
Allison, FitzSimons, 117
Allport, Gordon, 6
Ambrose, 43
Ammonius Saccas, 23, 26
Andrewes, Lancelot, 116-118
Angelico, Fra, 75
Anselm, 55, 57, 80, 123, 138, 160
Aquinas, Thomas, 66, 68-69, 72, 80, 97, 104, 113
Aristotle, 68-69, 72
Arndt, Johann, 136-137
Athanasius, 34
Auden, W. H., 119
Augustine of Canterbury, 46
Augustine of Hippo, 43-45, 55, 57-58, 62, 66, 72, 79, 87, 99, 108, 123, 125

Baker, Augustine, 85, 112, 123
Barfield, Owen, 86
Barlaam, 91
Barnabas, Epistle of, 21
Basil of Caesarea, 31

Baxter, Richard, 131, 132
Beatrice of Nazareth, 71
Bede, Venerable, 49
Bellarmine, Robert, 104
Benedict of Nursia, 46
Bernard of Clairvaux, 55-57, 62, 71, 79-80, 87, 99, 109, 113, 122, 129
Berulle, Pierre de, 108-109
Boehme, Jacob, 122, 123, 128-130, 132, 135, 140
Bonaventure, 49-50, 66-67, 72, 87, 102
Booty, John, 122
Bouyer, Louis, 31, 36, 41, 114, 116-117, 123, 129-131, 133, 135, 144
Brightman, Edgar, 155
Bruehl, Levy, 83
Bruno, 54
Bunyan, John, 122, 132-133

Cajetan (founder of Theatines), 104
Cajetan, Thomas de Vio (cardinal and theologian), 104
Calvin, John, 86, 104, 124, 127, 128, 130, 137

Cassian, John, 37, 45-46, 78
Castaneda, Carlos, 30, 79, 99
Catherine of Genoa, 86-88
Chantal, Jeanne de, *see* Jeanne de Chantal
Chrodegang of Metz, 52
Clare of Assisi, 106
Clement of Alexandria, 25-26, 34, 40
Cloud of Unknowing, The, 61, 76, 79-82, 101, 102, 112
Curé d'Ars, *see* Vianney, Jean-Baptiste Marie

Deikmann, Arthur, 6
deSales, Francis, *see* Francis de Sales
deWolf, Harold, 155
Diadochos of Photike, 35
Dionysius the pseudo-Areopagite, 31, 34, 38-40, 43, 49, 51-52, 55, 61-62, 66, 68, 72, 75, 79, 86, 99, 125
Dominic, 68, 150
Donne, John, 114-116, 118
Douglas, Mary, 9

Eckhart, Meister, 71-73, 75-76, 84, 125, 126, 151, 153
Edwards, Jonathan, 10, 138, 139, 140
Eliot, T. S., 80, 114, 119, 121
Erigena, John Scotus, 52-53, 57-58
Erikson, Erik, 12
Eudes, John, 109, 131
Evagrius Ponticus, 30, 36-40, 50, 88, 91, 143, 146

Fénelon, Francis, 107, 140
Ferrar, Nicholas, 120-121, 132
Fowler, James, 12
Fox, George, 135, 138

Francis de Sales, 105-107, 109, 113, 122, 138, 140
Francis of Assisi, 65-66, 150
Francke, August Hermann, 138
Fremantle, Anne, 119
Frost, Bede, 149

Gallus, Thomas, 61, 79
Gandhi, Mohandas, 155
Gerson, John, 86-87, 100, 128, 137
Giotto, 66
Goodwin, Thomas, 131
Graef, Hilda, 105
Gregory VII, 54
Gregory of Nazianzen, 31
Gregory of Nyssa, 27-28, 30-35, 39-40, 43-44, 52, 55, 57-58, 81, 88, 91, 99, 102, 115, 130, 138, 159
Gregory Palamas, 91-92
Gregory the Great, 48-49, 79
Groote, Gerard, 84
Guigo II, 54

Hadewijch of Antwerp, 71
Hammarskjöld, Dag, 150, 152, 153
Hart, Ray, 147
Harton, F. P., 149
Hegel, G. W. F., 130
Herbert, George, 114, 118-121, 127, 131, 151
Hermes Trismegistus, 23
Heschel, Abraham, 150
Hilton, Walter, 30, 79, 81-82, 112-113
Hoffman, Bengt, 105, 125-126
Hood, Ralph W., Jr., 6
Hooker, Richard, 112-113
Hopkins, Gerard Manley, 145

Hügel, Friederich von, see von
    Hügel, Friederich
Hugh of St. Victor, 60-63, 113
Husserl, Edmund, 145
Huxley, Aldous, 123
Hypatia, 41

Ignatius Loyola, 58, 67-68, 76,
    93-97, 107, 114, 124, 132,
    140, 159
Ignatius of Antioch, 22
Innocent XI, 110
Irenaeus of Lyons, 20, 22, 32, 99
Isaac of Nineveh, 38, 52
Isidore of Seville, 49

James, William, 107
Jansen, Cornelius, 108
Jeanne de Chantal, 106
Jerome, 43
Joachim of Fiore, 134
John Chrysostom, 41
John Climacus, 30, 37-38, 89-90
John of Fecamp, 54-55, 57
John of the Cross, 1-2, 79, 92,
    99-102, 107, 118, 131, 143,
    151-152, 158
John Scotus, see Erigena
John the Baptist, 17
John the Evangelist, 20
Jones, Rufus, 125, 135
Julian of Norwich, 59, 63, 79-82,
    113-114, 118, 122-123, 130,
    151
Jung, C. G., 38, 130

Kant, Immanuel, 142, 145
Keble, John, 144
Kempe, Margery, 83, 84, 114
Kierkegaard, Sören, 17, 152

King, Martin Luther, 151,
    155-157
Kirk, Kenneth, 48
Kohlberg, Lawrence, 12

Law, William, 96, 122-123, 140
Lewis, C. S., 130
Little Flower, see Therese of Lisieux
Lonergan, Bernard, 59
Louis IX, 10
Loyola, see Ignatius Loyola
Lull, Raymond, 67-68, 76
Luther, Martin, 36, 63, 73, 85,
    124-127, 129, 134

Macarius, 35-36
Marlow, Abraham, 107
Maximus the Confessor, 49-50, 52,
    89-90
Merton, Thomas, 56, 84, 112,
    153-155
Molina, Luis de, 104
Molinos, Miguel de, 107, 110
Moses, 27
Münzer, Thomas, 134-135

Neilos of Ancyra, 35
Neri, Philip, 108
Newman, John Henry, 110, 144
Nicodemus of the Holy Mountain,
    146-147
Nicholas of Basle, 73

Oberman, Heiko, 126
Olier, Jean-Jacques, 108, 118, 149
Origen, 25-29, 32-33, 36, 40-41,
    50, 55, 57-58, 65, 131, 138

Pascal, Blaise, 110-111
Patrick, 50

Paul, 18-19, 22, 30, 32, 34, 36, 40, 108, 159
Percy, William Alexander, 156
Philemon, Abba, 35
Philo, 16-18, 27, 30, 32-33, 38, 40, 50
Piaget, Jean, 12
Plato, 30, 68, 72
Plotinus, 23-24, 26
Poimandres, 23
Polycarp, 21
Procus, 39
Pseudo-Macarius, 35-37, 79, 91
Pusey, Edward, 144

Rabanus Maurus, 51
Rahner, Karl, 32
Rauschenbush, Walter, 155
Richard, Lucien Joseph, 128
Richard of St. Victor, 60-64, 68, 79, 86, 99, 113
Richelieu, Cardinal, 108
Ricouer, Paul, 86, 145, 160
Ritschl, Albrech, 143
Robinson, J. A. T., 129
Rolle, Richard, 45, 77-79, 81, 85, 130
Rous, Francis, 130-131
Ruysbroeck, John, 75-76, 84, 99, 122

Savonarola, Jerome, 104
Scupoli, Lawrence, 104
Second Hadewijch, 71, 75
Shepherd of Hermas, 21
Simeon the New Theologian, 90
Simon, New Testament Theologian, 38
Solomon, 27
Spener, Phillipp Jakob, 136-137

Stoeffler, Ernest, 137
Suso, Henry, 75
Synesius of Cyrene, 41-42

Tatian 21-22
Tauler, John, 63, 71-75, 84, 122, 125, 126, 134-135
Taylor, Jeremy, 117-118
Teresa of Avila, 93, 98-99, 102, 140
Tersteegen, Gerhard, 143-145
Tertullian, 57, 134
Theophan the Recluse, 105, 147-148
Therese of Lisieux, 144-145
Thomas à Kempis, 55, 85, 99, 122
Thomas Aquinas, see Aquinas, Thomas
Thornton, Martin, 77, 80, 82, 114, 117, 118-119, 121-122, 129, 130, 144
Thoth, 23
Tillich, Paul, 129
Turner, Victor, 7

Underhill, Evelyn, 80, 148-149
Urban II, 54

Vanderbroucke, Francois, 82
Vane, Harry, 132
Vaughan-Williams, Ralph, 119
Vianney, Jean-Baptiste Marie, 144
von Hügel, Friederich, 143, 145-146, 148

Walton, Izaak, 121
Weber, Max, 127
Weil, Simone, 119, 151-152, 154
Wesley, Charles, 141

Wesley, John, 10, 36, 122, 130, 140-43

Whelan, Joseph, 146

Whitefield, George, 10, 122, 140-141

Wilberforce, William, 144

William of Ockham, 70

William of St. Thierry, 53, 56-59, 67, 76, 80-81, 123

Woolman, John, 139-140

Ximenes de Cisneros, Garcia, 93, 132

Zinzendorf, Ludwig Graf von, 140

Zinzendorf, Nikolaus, 109

Zwingli, Ulrich, 124